One Good Man

Rev. John Lamb Prichard's life of faith, service and sacrifice

by Rev. J.D. Hufham
edited by Jack E. Fryar, Jr.

New Hanover County Public Library
201 Chestnut Street
Wilmington, North Carolina 28401

Originally published in 1867 as
*Memoir of Rev. John L. Prichard, late Pastor of the First Baptist Church,
Wilmington, N.C.*

First Edition 1867
Published in the United States of America by Dram Tree Books.

Publisher's Cataloging-in-Publication Data
(Provided by DRT Press)

Hufham, James Dunn, 1834-1921
   One good man : Rev. John Lamb Prichard's life of faith, service and sacrifice / by Rev. J.D. Hufham ; edited by Jack E. Fryar, Jr.
      p. cm
      ISBN 0-9786248-8-2
   "Originally published in 1867 as Memoir of John L. Prichard, late Pastor of the First Baptist Church, Wilmington, N.C."

1. Prichard, John Lamb, 1811-1862. 2. North Carolina--Biography. 3. Virginia--Biography. 4. Baptists--Biography. 5. Clergy--Biography. 7. First Baptist Church (Wilmington, N.C.). 6. United States History Civil War, 1861-1865. I. Fryar, Jack E. II. Title.

BX6495.P75 H8 2007
921-dc22

10 9 8 7 6 5 4 3 2 1

Dram Tree Books
P.O. Box 7183
Wilmington, N.C. 28406
(910) 538-4076
www.dramtreebooks.com
Potential authors: visit our website or email us for submission guidelines

Volume discounts available.
Call or e-mail for terms.

Preface to the 2007 Edition

John Lamb Prichard was a man whose faith dictated his every move. He lived in times that demanded much of people, and the challenges and sacrifices Lamb faced must surely have tested the strength of his beliefs. The most dramatic episodes of Prichard's life came at the end, when he was leading the congregation at Wilmington, N.C.'s First Baptist Church. He lost a wife. He saw the country lurching towards the crisis that would result in the bloodiest war in our nation's history. He braved a terrible scourge that would take the lives of one third of the residents of North Carolina's largest city, until it finally claimed Prichard, too.

Perhaps Rev. Prichard's finest hour came during that deadly epidemic of 1862, when the air of Wilmington reeked of turpentine from burning smoke pots and wagons carried their grim burdens to Oakdale Cemetery on a daily basis. When yellow fever made its presence known in Wilmington, those who could evacuated to the surrounding countryside, where they hoped to be out of reach of the mysterious killer. Rev. Prichard and two other men of faith were the only ones who chose to remain to comfort the dying and their families. The disease eventually killed two of those men of God, and John Lamb Prichard was one of them.

But while death deprived Wilmington of one of its best citizens, Prichard had one last gift for those who came after him. He was a devoted letter writer and diarist, and in those missives we learn the story of this man who put his faith into action, even at the cost of his own life. Prichard's eloquent words remain one of our best accounts of what happened in Wilmington during that terrible summer and fall of 1862. After the war, Prichard's friend, Rev. J.D. Hufham, collected those letters and diaries and the reminiscences of those who knew him, to publish this memorial to the late minister. It is a story of faith, service and sacrifice that serves as an inspiration for people of faith today, exemplifying what it means to have the courage of one's convictions. This book is a tribute to John Lamb Prichard, and the story of one good man.

Jack E. Fryar, Jr.
Wilmington, N.C.
2007

PREFACE

The little volume, which is now offered to the public, was to have been issued soon after Mr. Prichard's death while his name, his virtues and his labors were fresh in the minds of the people. The work has been delayed by several causes, principally by the difficulties experienced in collecting the materials which make up the Memoir, while the war was raging.

It may be, however, that the delay will be rather advanageous than otherwise, so far as the accomplishment of good is concerned. It is believed that the record of an earnest life, as set forth in the following pages, has a peculiar adaptation to the times in which we live; and that young men especially—those who are now taking their first lessons in adversity, as well as those who, like Mr. P., have been struggling with poverty since childhood—may study that record with advantage.

The profits accruing from the sale of the book, will be applied to the education of Mr. P's. children. If it shall accomplish anything in this direction, and shall be instrumental in quickening the spiritual life of any who read it, by stimulating them to newness of hope and effort, the object in preparing and publishing it will have been accomplished.

James Dunn Hufham
RALEIGH, N. C., 1867.

CONTENTS

MEMOIR OF

REV. J. L. PRICHARD.

Reverend John Lamb Prichard not long before his death of yellow fever.

CHAPTER I.

BIRTH—EARLY CHILDHOOD—FIRST AFFLICTION—REVERSE
OF FORTUNE—EARLY STRUGGLES—MATERNAL INFLUENCE—
CONVERSION—CHRISTIAN DEVOTION—THOUGHTS OF THE
MINISTRY.

JOHN LAMB PRICHARD was born in Pasquotank county, N. C., on
the 6th of June 1811, and was the second of six children. There was
little either in his appearance, during his earlier years, or in the
condition of his family, to indicate the commanding influence and eminent
usefulness to which he afterwards attained. His parents were in moderate
circumstances, possessing enough property, with the aid of industry and
economy, to furnish them a comfortable living. They saw and desired to
see little of fashion's gay throng and were strangers to the luxuries which
wealth brings in its train.

But they had what is far better, contentment with their lot, and a
quiet, unobtrusive yet earnest piety. Both were members of a Baptist
church, and by their blameless lives won the confidence and esteem of all

who knew them. Mr. Prichard used to relate that his father would arise a great while before day in order that he might have opportunity to study the Scriptures and offer praise and prayer to God before entering on his regular routine of labor. It is also known that he was a liberal and unselfish man, always ready to relieve the sufferings of others, without reference to his own comfort or convenience.

His wife was a fit companion for him. Industrious and frugal, always careful to provide the physical comforts of home for her family, she still kept their spiritual interests uppermost in her mind, and strove, by her example, her precepts and her prayers, to lead her children to Christ. Her maternal faithfulness had a rich reward even here; for she lived to see them all consistent and useful christians. Four of them have passed away from the earth, and within a recent period she has gone to join them in a brighter, happier sphere.

In this peaceful, happy home, surrounded by these gracious influences, the first nine years of Mr. Prichard's life were spent. What wonder that his memory should often have reverted to this brief sunny period, amid the struggles and sorrows of his later years, or, young as he was, that it should have been protential in shaping the whole of his subsequent career? He was growing up a delicate boy, of slender frame, ardent temperament and social disposition, yet having a keen relish for active out-door sports, and by enquiry and observation already laying the foundation for the stores of knowledge which he afterwards accumulated. As yet he knew nothing of real trials or sorrows. But God, when He would prepare His servants for some great work, not unfrequently carries them first through a course of discipline in the stern school of suffering, and Mr. Prichard's term of pupilage was about to commence.

When he had reached his ninth year, death came into the household and tore the husband and father from hearts that clung to him with agonizing tenderness. On the subject of this memoir the event made a deep and lasting impression. To the close of his life he remembered his feelings "when aroused from sleep at night to see the best of fathers die." This first great family grief was rendered more poignant by what followed. The liberality and kind-heartedness of the elder Prichard has been alluded to. He had become surety for several persons and after his death most of his property was sold to pay their debts.

Her husband laid in the grave, the widow with the remnant of her little fortune and her six children, the oldest of them but eleven years of age, left the scene of her purest, sweetest joys and of her keenest sufferings, and returned to Camden county, where she had been reared and where most of her kindred still resided. Here she settled and commenced life anew. Her lot seemed hard, but her trust in God was firm and unwavering and she neither murmured nor desponded.

It will be a suitable tribute to the memory of this excellent woman to refer to the patient endurance and the cheerful application to the discharge of duty which distinguished her in the painful circumstances in which she was thrown. These attributes were marked in her character. Is it too much to believe, that besides the influence of a natural buoyancy of spirit, the widow's God imparted peculiar, supernatural wisdom and strength, to qualify her for the new trials and responsibilities of her position? The promises of the Bible addressed to the widow and orphan, are perhaps more numerous and explicit, than to any other class of afflicted ones. Is it then surprising that Mrs. Prichard, borne down by the pressure of heavy calamity, and out of the depths of her sorrow, looking up to the God of her salvation, should have been upheld and sustained?

Labor was a necessity both to her and her children. John was employed on the farm a while, but afterwards choosing a vocation more in accordance with his character and tastes, he served an apprenticeship as a house-carpenter. The terms of his contract were faithfully observed, and it was a matter of principle with him to do neatly and with dispatch whatever he undertook—characteristics which he maintained through life.

Many evidences of his skill and industry are still to be seen in the region where he lived. Nor was he ever ashamed to refer to the fact that his earlier years were spent at the plough and in the work-shop. In one or two instances members of his congregation, with a feeling of worldly pride, manifested a restless uneasiness lest their position in society should be injured by these references of their pastor. He however shared not such feelings and for the purpose of elucidating some truth or enforcing some duty would often introduce in his discourses, allusions to the time of his apprenticeship. Referring too, to visits afterwards made to Camden, he would advert with satisfaction to buildings more or less important which had risen under his direction.

For the encouragement of the young, especially of young ministers, he would point to the way along which God had led him, deeming it no disgrace to himself or his ministry that his earlier years had been spent in toilsome employments.

Although, during the whole of his youth and early manhood he labored constantly at his trade, it did not quench his thirst for knowledge. At night and in the brief intervals of leisure he eagerly perused such books as came within his reach, adding to his stock of information and forming the habit of reading which he ever afterwards retained.

His ardent temperament and social disposition led him, at this period, to enter with zest into the amusements common to persons of his age, and he afterwards deeply deplored the frivolities in which he then indulged.

In 1831, when he was twenty years old, the great event of his life occurred. The good seed sown in his heart by parental instruction and example sprung into life under the blessing of God and brought forth fruit. He was happily and thoroughly converted, and was baptized into the fellowship of the church at Shiloh, Camden county, by Rev. Evan Forbes. His convictions were deep and pungent and his sufferings intense, while he was groping his way slowly through the darkness of ignorance and unbelief. Light came suddenly, and with it ecstatic joy and perfect peace of mind. So clearly marked was the work of grace in his heart that the time and the place where his sufferings were relieved were indelibly impressed on his memory. In the free interchange of thought and feeling which he held with those he loved and trusted, he used to tell, with trembling lips, how he went to a solitary place to pray, bowed down under a load of guilt, distressed by fearful forebodings and brought to the verge of despair; how, as he poured out his soul before God, he was enabled to accept Christ as his Ransom, his Mediator, his Portion, his all; and how joy and peace unutterable filled his soul.

It was doubtless due to his experience of the preciousness of Christ and the plan of salvation, in this the hour of his conversion, that throughout his ministerial life he dwelt so much and so urgently on the simplicity and efficacy of the gospel as the only foundation of human hope. His views of this system, and its adaptation to human necessity, seem to have been remarkably clear.

It is, too, an interesting fact that his conversion occurred during a season of religious excitement in the community which continued many months, and which resulted in large accessions to the churches of that region. The idea is sometimes entertained, that such a season is unfavorable to intelligent apprehensions of spiritual truth. But it will be found that more depends on the judgment and fidelity of those who conduct these seasons, than on a mere freedom from excitement. Thus while the subject of this memoir was in the midst of influences peculiarly exciting, he failed not to apprehend in a large degree those doctrinal truths which lie at the basis of all true religion.

Though his christian experience was so clear in its earlier stages, he was not without sore temptations and trials afterwards. He mentioned among other things, that he was strongly tempted to use profane oaths. "Sometimes," he said, "I was afraid to open my mouth lest I should swear in spite of myself." Doubts and fears came now and then, but they were only the ripples which appear on the surface of the lake. The hidden depths of trust and hope, far beyond the reach of the adversary, maintained an unbroken calm.

Now commences that career of christian activity and usefulness which for more than thirty years had no intermission. As soon as he accepted Christ he began to talk and to labor for Christ. The region in which he lived, continued to enjoy the gracious revival of religion already referred to, more than a year. It was the custom to hold prayer-meetings from house to house through the neighborhood. Mr. Prichard regularly attended these meetings and often conducted them. After working all day at his trade he would walk three or four miles, and even farther, in order that he might have his own soul refreshed and, if opportunity was offered, speak a word for Jesus. Nor did he confine his efforts to these public meetings. He never failed, when he could do it, to present the claims of religion to those whom he met in the walks of his daily life. The church at Shiloh esteemed him so highly that they called him to the deaconship and in this office he served them acceptably till he was led into another and wider field of usefulness.

In subsequent life, Mr. Prichard frequently referred with deep interest to the scenes and circumstances familiar to him at this period. Those night meetings, so frequent and refreshing, he never forgot. Along the public thorough fare and more retired pathways he was accustomed to pass, on his way to these religious gatherings, he employed the time in the contemplation of the Lord's ways, and in meditation on his word. Often, as he then mused, the word of the Lord was like fire in his bones, and he could not restrain himself. Is it not wonderful that reaching the social meeting, he should give vent to the pent up feelings of his soul, nor, that in these hortotary appeals, he should have given promise of future usefulness in the ministery.

His thoughts, at this time, were occasionally directed to the duty of preaching the Gospel, but it was not till several years afterwards, while pursuing his studies at Wake Forest College, that he decided to enter on the work. Doubtless he was restrained from an immediate devotion to the ministry by a sense of personal unfitness. His views of responsibility in this department of christian labor, were somewhat peculiar. The momentous issues, for weal or woe, growing out of the office, and the high qualifications essential to the right performance of its duties, prepared him to shrink from it. He thought too, it would not be right for him to preach, without more of preparation by mental culture, and enlarged general, as well as Scriptural knowledge. It were well if more of this solemn dread of rushing uncalled into a work so important were entertained by the young men of the churches. Then with earnest beseechings for Divine education would they approach the mercy seat, and with more of assiduity and perseverance would they seek the attainments requisite to becoming able ministers of the New Testament. Thus it seemed to be with Mr. Prichard.

His thirst for information continued unabated. Before, he had sought it in order that he might improve his worldly condition. Now he desired it for a higher, nobler purpose—that he might be more extensively useful. He longed to take a regular course of study, but this seemed impossible. He was poor, dependent on his daily labor for food and raiment; he had no wealthy or influential friends to take him by the hand or smooth his pathway; schools were few and expensive and books were not then so cheap and abundant as they have since become. How could his heart's desire be gratified? There seemed to be little ground for hope. And yet the day was fixed when, by God's blessing on a childlike faith and an unyielding will, knowledge should unfold to his delighted vision "her ample page rich with the spoils of time."

CHAPTER II.

BAPTISTS OF NORTH CAROLINA PREVIOUS TO 1830—
EXTENSIVE REVIVALS—ORIGIN OF THE BAPTIST STATE
CONVENTION—PROMINENT MOVERS—WAKE FOREST
INSTITUTE—AGENCY OF MR. ARMSTRONG—MR. PRICHARD
ENTERS THE INSTITUTION—CHARACTER AS A STUDENT—
HIS TRIALS—GRADUATION.

Until the year 1830, the Baptists of North Carolina were without an organization which had for its object to bring the whole denomination in the State into harmonious and efficient co-operation in the work of spreading the Gospel. For a few years there was a Missionary Society, but it did not last long and its operations were confined to a small portion of the State. There was also a "General Meeting for correspondence," but it was not a Missionary body. Neither had the district Associations adopted the present plan of attempting to supply the destitution of the home field through Boards of their own. In a few cases ministers were instructed to labor as evangelists and a specified sum was raised for them by public collections. By far the greater part of the missionary work of those early days was performed by the churches and their pastors. Many of the churches had out-stations, which were visited by the pastor or some member of the church, and services were held in school-houses, private residences, or the open air, as circumstances required. Many of these out-stations exist to this day—out-stations no longer, but flourishing and self-sustaining churches. It was the custom of the pastors to obtain leave of absence from their churches for weeks or months, and make protracted journeys through the country, preaching at night or during the day, wherever the people could be gathered together. Commencing at the home of some family willing to hear the Gospel, they labored from house to house till whole neighborhoods were converted to God and churches were organized where preaching had previously been almost unknown.

Those who scattered the seeds of which we are reaping the harvest were little versed in the learning of the schools. Plain men called to this holy work from secular pursuits, they brought to the study of the English Bible, large, round-about common sense and a spirit of earnest prayer and humble dependence in God. They went forth, impelled by the love of the Redeemer which was burning within them, guided in their movements by what they termed their "impressions" and by the indications of Providence, and labored without pecuniary reward. Indeed they did not expect this. They received only the free-will offerings of the communities in which they preached. How little this was, is demonstrated by the poverty in which most of them lived and died.

Their sermons would hardly stand the test of criticism according to the standards of to-day, but they were rich in Gospel truth, presented in language and enforced by arguments and illustrations which at once took hold on the popular mind. They dealt largely in christian experience, and in their exhortations and appeals there was a fire, an unction, which at times made them almost irresistible. Under their ministry revivals prevailed, which in extent and power have too few parallels now. They frequently extended through the greater portion of a year, or two years, in the same section of country and the number of souls added to the churches during their continuance was truly wonderful.

Through the ministry of these men the multiplication of Baptist churches and the spread of Baptist sentiments in the State were remarkably rapid. From one church in 1727, and one Association in 1758, they were to be found at the period of which we write, in all parts of the State.

The time for concert of action among the Baptists of North Carolina had now come. The preliminary meeting was held in Greenville, in 1830, and the first session of the Baptist State Convention of North Carolina was held in 1831, with the church at Cross-Roads, Wake county.—There were present forty delegates from thirty six churches and seventeen counties. The object of the Convention was the promotion of home and foreign missions and of ministerial education, and the collections for this purpose, during the year, were $819.90.

Many of the members were pioneers such as we have described above, but men of large souls and liberal views. Most of them have since gone to their reward, but

> *"The memory of their virtues lingers yet,*
> *Like soft twilight hues when the sun is set."*

It is pleasant to find, among them the names of such men as John Purefoy, Q. H. Trotman, George M. Thompson, W. P. Biddle, Eli Philips, George Fennell and Job Goodman. They were a tower of strength in their day.

It will not be understood that there was any real incongruity between the spirit and labors of these noble men, and of those who succeeded them. They were eminently adapted to the times in which they lived. Anything like state action, or general combination, would have been exceedingly inconvenient, if not impossible. The benefits of the printing press were but little enjoyed. Mail facilities were infrequent and uncertain. Railroads were things unthought of, and communication with distant places, even by the stage coach, was expensive and irregular. In the earlier history of the Triennial Baptist Convention, Jesse Mercer was, by necessity, compelled to travel from his home in Georgia to Philadelphia or New York by private conveyance. To make such a journey was an event in those days. It is said that this devoted man on the Lord's day before his departure from home found himself surrounded by weeping crowds, sorrowing most of all, lest they should see his face no more. It must not be assumed therefore that the fathers in their sacrifices and toils were animated by a spirit which is not breathed by their sons, or that the latter in their superior advantages of position are governed by a more elevated devotion to the cause of Jesus.

But in this assembly there were some men of liberal culture. First among these we mention Rev. Samuel Wait, D. D., then a young man fresh from college and the Theological Seminary, full of enthusiasm and energy, wise in laying plans and patient in executing them. One of the most prominent and active among the originators of the Convention he identified himself thoroughly with it, canvassed the State for it, striving by every means in his power to enlist all the churches in its support, and for more than thirty years gave to it his contributions, his labors and his prayers. He still lingers, honored and loved, amid the scenes of his earlier years, quietly awaiting the summons home.

Rev. John Armstrong was a valuable co-laborer in the new movement. More scholarly but less impassioned than Dr. Wait, he brought to the consideration of every question a clear head and a strong will. He settled in North Carolina as a teacher, was afterwards pastor of the church in Newbern, then Corresponding Secretary of the Convention and agent for the Institute at Wake Forest. For a short time he filled a Professor's chair in the Institute, but went to Paris to prepare himself better for the discharge of his duties. Subsequently he removed to Columbus, Mississippi, and there died.

Rev. Thomas Meredith was also there. He was educated for the law, but God had a nobler work for him. Having been converted to God he entered the ministry and settled in this State as pastor of the church in Edenton. There he published the *Baptist Interpeter,* a monthly, and the first Baptist periodical ever issued in North Carolina. Subsequently he was called to the pastorate in Newbern and there the *Interpreter* was changed into the *Biblical Recorder,* a weekly newspaper. To extend its circulation and increase its usefulness he removed to Raleigh and there remained till the close of his life. A man of dignified and commanding presence, a fluent speaker, a clear and forcible reasoner, and thoroughly informed on all the topics of the day, he at once took a high rank among the Baptists of the State. Nor did it stop here. His power as a writer was fully equal to that which was conceded to him as a speaker. At different times he was brought into collision with many of the first men, not only of his own denomination but also among the Pedobaptists. It is needless to say that he proved himself a match for the ablest of his opponents. A laborious man through the whole of his life, all his wealth of influence and knowledge and intellect was devoted to the promotion of the Baptist cause. He sleeps in the cemetery in Raleigh, and a monument erected by his brethren marks his resting-place and indicates the estimation in which he was held.

If it were proper to speak of those who still remain, "abundant in labors" as in days of yore, honorable mention might be made of Rev. W. Hooper, D.D., L.L.D., whose praise is in all the churches, and of Rev. James McDaniel who, for seventeen years, has presided over the deliberations of the body in whose organization he bore an active part.

By such men the Convention was organized. Their views were liberal and their plans were large, reaching far out into the future. They encountered opposition, but met it fearlessly yet wisely, and were permitted to see it give way before them and the whole denomination in the State, nominally at least, enlisted with them in the great enterprises which they originated.

Let it not be supposed that these are mere useless details thrown in to fill up space. They are necessary to a proper estimate of the subject of this memoir. His earlier experiences were among the pioneer laborers mentioned at the beginning of this chapter. Under the ministry of one of them, and in one of those remarkable revivals which characterized that period of our denominational history, he was converted to God. His dawning manhood witnessed and entered into the new order of things, and the principal actors were his instructors or his cherished friends and advisers. He carried with him through life many of the best elements of both periods. His piety was strongly marked and experimental in its character. He had great fondness and aptitude for the work of the home missionary and colporter, while he was equally happy and successful in the settled life of the pastor. He had all the earnestness of manner and plainness of speech of the fathers, with the study and research of a later day.

The promotion of education, especially among the rising ministry, was one of the primary objects of the Convention. At its first session two young brethren were received as beneficiaries and sent to schools of established reputation. At the second session a committee of which Rev. W. Hooper, D.D., L.L.D., was Chairman, recommended the purchase of a suitable farm and the establishment of a school for young men "on the manual labor principle." The plan was, to allow the young men to work a certain number of hours each day at a stipulated price. It was hoped that many would thus be enabled to secure the advantages of education, who would otherwise be deprived of them forever. It was thought that they might at least pay their board in this way.

The farm was purchased and in 1834 Wake Forest Institute went into operation under the supervision of Dr. Wait. In may 1834, Rev. John Armstrong took the field as agent of the Institute. On one of his trips through the Eastern part of the State he made the acquaintance of Mr. Prichard, then working as a carpenter with his brother. He became interested in the young man, drew from him his short, sad history, his desires, his poverty, his hopes, his fears. Mr. Armstrong related a portion of his own history—told him how through his childhood and youth he toiled in poverty and obscurity at the trade of a tinner, and how by perseverance and the favor of God he had risen to the position which he then occupied—and his listener at length promised to go to the Institute after he had finished the house on which he and his brother were then engaged. That house is still standing and there are those yet living who remember the hour when, his work completed, he threw down his hammer, saying in his emphatic way, "This is my last job here. I am now going to school." Some of his companions in study and labor also remember his arrival at the Institute at night, with his scanty wardrobe, his tools and such books as he had been able to gather together.

He entered the Institution about the middle of 1835. Here new employments and new trials awaited him. He was to retain his old habits to some extent, for he had little money and on the labor of his hands depended the one cherished purpose of his heart. Yet for a part of each day he must be another man, must change his habits and become a student— no easy task certainly. The history of his inner life at this period would be interesting and profitable. Unfortunately he has left behind him few memorials of its struggles and triumphs; and we must judge of it by the fruits which afterwards appeared and by the statements of his teachers and his fellow students. That he faithfully attended to his studies is evident from the accuracy and extent of his knowledge in later years and the habits which he carried with him to the close of his life. Few men had a larger fund of general information. Few preachers are more careful in their preparation for the pulpit. This would not have been the case had he not laid a good foundation while he was a student at Wake Forest.

That he worked with his hands is also well known. Even the vacations brought no rest for him. They were precious seasons, however, as by plying his trade through their brief, fleeting days and weeks he was enabled to earn something with which to meet the expenses of the next session. During one of these vacations he laid the floor of the dining-room of the Institute; and there are some houses still standing, monuments of his earnestness and conscientiousness. He tenderly loved his mother and sisters. Yet he visited them but twice during his college course. Time and money were too precious to be diverted from the great object which he had in view.

College life is usually a trying season to the young christian. Many who are consistent and active servants of the Master at home, are either silent amid the unholy revelry of gay companions or are drawn with them into the paths of folly and sin. Not so with Mr. Prichard. There was no decline in his spirituality, no irregularity in his private devotions, no neglect of his public duties. In the Sabbath school and the prayer-meeting he always bore his part. More than once during his stay there, the Institute was visited with revivals of religion. During these gracious seasons there was no one whose counsel and sympathy and prayers were more eagerly sought than those of Mr. Prichard.

The following testimonials concerning him at this period of his life will be read with interest. Dr. Wait, his venerated instructor and friend, writes:

"It is but just to state that from the commencement of his course of study at Wake Forest, he was the *christian student.* He seemed never to forget that he had consecrated himself to God in baptism; that he was not his own; that he had been bought with a price and must therefore glorify God in both body and spirit. Hence in all his exhibitions in the chapel, whether, in the earlier part of his course, he used for declamation the thoughts of another, or whether, when farther advanced, he used only original compositions, he was sure to say something in favor of religion.

From a circumstance which I have heard him relate more than once in the course of our long acquaintance, I think he did not decide that it was his duty to preach the gospel till near the close of his college course. He and a classmate, who also entered the ministry, had charge of a Sabbath school about one mile from the college for two years. On the occasion referred to they closed the school with an address and prayer. Our departed brother informed me that while speaking to the children, some of them very small, he often saw the starting tear, and other indications that what he said was understood and felt. This circumstance settled the point. He felt that he must preach."

Prof. W. T. Brooks, who was his intimate friend then and through life, writes:

"He came here when the manual labor system was in operation, expecting to work his way through college. And this he strove to do, using his plane and saw a part of the time, and poring over his books when not thus engaged. His progress was rapid, for he knew the value of time and thirsted for knowledge. He was universally esteemed by his fellow-students. All had confidence in him as a christian, and in difficulties many sought his advice. The younger students looked up to him as to an elder brother and always found him ready to sympathize with them in trouble or to redress their wrongs. He was always on the side of good order and his influence in this particular was most happy.

His efforts to sustain himself by his own exertions were not entirely successful, even while the manual labor system was retained. It was abolished before the completion of his course and then he was reduced to great straits by want of funds. But the Hand that had led him thus far sustained him in this season of trial. A friend who suspected his condition came forward voluntarily and relieved him. This difficulty returned at intervals till near the close of his stay here when the Board of the Convention gave him such assistance as he needed."

The following letter throws light on the statement of Prof. Brooks:

WAKE FOREST INSTITUTE, Feb. 8th, 1837.

DEAR SIR:—I trust I shall find an excuse, in your kind feelings, for the liberty I take in addressing you. From a conversation I had this afternoon with Professor Armstrong, I am induced to believe that a communication from me would not be altogether unexpected by you.

I have always felt an unquenchable thirst for knowledge and have been willing to make any sacrifice to obtain it; but my very limited pecuniary means have presented obstacles, which I have never been able to overcome. When the Wake Forest Institute was put in operation, a new hope sprung up in my bosom. I persuaded myself that I should be able by my labor to meet the expenses of an education. With this view, I entered the Institute about two years ago. But alas! my hopes have been disappointed. I am now in debt to the Institute, and my labor is far from being adequate to meet my expenses. My immediate relatives, you know, are poor, and where to look for aid, but to yourself, I know not. I am now *in the College department and have four years to remain before I can graduate. Must I now give up all hope of an education? The very idea, to me, is as bitter as the dying struggle. Will you be my kind friend? With the blessing of God upon me, you shall not lose, by your kindness, one cent. I am persuaded that I shall be able to return with interest all that my education may require, within eighteen months after I shall have graduated. I am now in debt to the Institute, $116.27. If, in addition to this sum, I can obtain $100 a year for four years, I shall obtain the most ardent wish of my heart. I shall make my labor help me in procuring clothes and books. Dear sir, will you befriend me? Will you become the most valuable friend I can have on earth? O sir, I shall be bound to you by an affection that can never can cool, by gratitude that never can change.*

With profound respect, &c.

JNO. L. PRICHARD.

Little need be added to the extracts and to the letter which are given above. Brief as they are, they contain volumes. They set before us the picture of an earnest young man engaged in the pursuit of knowledge under the most serious difficulties and embarrassments. A stern sense of duty and a burning desire to rise in the scale of intelligence and usefulness urging him forward; poverty standing, like a lion grim and gaunt, in his path to turn him back. The story of those years—that struggle with the mind so often recurring, the effort, so often made and at last successful, to gain the mastery over it; those hours and days of severe physical labor, when the thoughts would steal away from the plane and saw and hammer to the text-book and the approaching recitation; the careful husbanding of money, and the intense anxiety and the agonizing prayer when it was all gone; the over whelming joy and thankfulness when relief came unexpectedly; the temptation to give up; the bitter feeling, so often repressed but so often returning, as young men more favored passed his place of trial with laugh and song and jest; the steady pursuit of the object, notwithstanding these things, and the final triumph;—this if it could be written would make a volume of thrilling interest, and one full of instruction and encouragement to many in all parts of the land.

All through this trying period, Prof. Armstrong was his friend and counsellor. Others sympathized with him in his struggles and sorrows, and advanced money from time to time. The kindness was remembered with fervent gratitude and the money was returned with scrupulous exactness.

There is little reason to doubt that the trials that beset Mr. Prichard, during his college life, were eminently sanctified in preparing him for more extensive usefulness in his Master's service. They proved a wholesome discipline, by which he learned to sympathize with the sons of poverty and toil, and especially with such young men as were compelled to wade through difficulties in their educational course. Then too he was the better fitted for the peculiar trials of the ministry. He had learned during his college life to endure hardness as a good soldier of Jesus Christ, so that no privations or sacrifices were sufficient to deter him from the prosecution of what he conceived to be his duty.

In this aspect of the subject, he was always accustomed in later years to recognize the trials of his student life as a part of his training necessary to his proper entrance upon the great work before him.

The period was now reached when the privations and toils of several years were to be repaid by the completion of the collegiate course. In 1840 he graduated with honor to himself, and to the institution of which he was a member. With buoyant heart he stepped forth from the halls of recitation, not to recline on a bed of ease or to luxuriate in the pleasures of social life, or even to gratify his taste and increase his general knowledge of men and things by travel, but, to labor in the vineyard of the Lord.

CHAPTER III.

REMOVAL TO MURFREESBORO, NORTH CAROLINA—LABORS
IN THE SCHOOL ROOM—VISIT TO MILTON—PREACHING IN
NORTH CAROLINA AND VIRGINIA—REV. JOHN KERR—
SETTLEMENT IN DANVILLE—ORDINATION—MARRIAGE—
EXTENSIVE LABORS—REVIVAL—PROTRACTED MEETING AT
BETHANY—CONSTITUTION OF BETHANY CHURCH—ROANOKE
ASSOCIATION—INFLUENCE IN FAVOR OF MISSIONS—
EXTRACTS FROM LETTERS.

We have seen Mr. Prichard a child in the seclusion of his early home; a youth, laboring at his trade through all the years of his apprenticeship; a student, striving to obtain the mastery of himself and to acquire that knowledge and those habits which would fit him for usefulness in after life, and waging all the while a fierce warfare with poverty. His faithfulness, earnestness, and unwavering fixedness of purpose and his final triumph have been set forth in the preceding pages. We are now to contemplate him in the arena of real life, where so many

who start with greater advantages and fairer prospects either fail
ingloriously or fall far short of the goal to which their own ambition and
the fond hopes of admiring friends point them.

With that foresight which stern experience had made habitual to
him he had been looking out for a field of labor before the completion of
his college course. At one time his thoughts were directed to the great
West which was then attracting so many of the unfortunate and the
adventurous from the Atlantic States. But God had already prepared a
place for him in a region nearer his old home.

As already noted, he graduated in June, 1840, and in July of the
same year became the principal of a large school in Murfreesboro. His
health, impaired by the labors and trials through which he had passed
while at Wake Forest, required rest and recreation, but some debts
necessarily contracted during his student-life rendered idleness, even for a
short time, an impossibility with him. These debts must be paid. He could
not even give himself wholly to the ministry, which he had now decided to
enter, till this was done. The thought of dependence, or of placing himself
in a position which might in any way compromise or tarnish his reputation
for honesty he could not brook for a moment. From his purpose to
discharge his pecuniary obligations fully and promptly, nothing could
divert him. Several situations which would have been eagerly accepted by
men of less conscientiousness and devotion to principle were offered him,
but he resolutely though respectfully declined them.

He remained in Murfreesboro a year, devoting himself to his
school during the week and preaching as opportunities were presented in
the surrounding country on the Sabbath. Arrangements had been made to
spend still another year in this place, but the field prepared for him by
Providence and already white unto harvest was awaiting him and to it he
must go. Failing health compelled him at last to seek recreation in the up-
country. While in Raleigh, with this object in view, in July 1841, he
formed the acquaintance of N. J. Palmer, Esq., of Milton, for many years
one of the most liberal and active Baptists of North Carolina. He invited
Mr. Pritchard to his home and the invitation was accepted. He remained
several weeks in the beautiful and healthful region adjacent to Milton,
enjoying the lavish and genial hospitality everywhere extended to him and
preaching every Sabbath. He went to Danville, Va., among other places,
and there formed the acquaintance of Rev. John Kerr. That venerable
servant of God, burdened with the weight of years and desiring to be

relieved of the active duties of the ministry, urged Mr. Prichard to remove to Danville, become an inmate of his house and accept the care of the church in that place. This pressing invitation, enforced by solicitations from adjacent communities which he had visited, was finally accepted. A union was thus formed which continued for years and was attended by the happiest results. Mr. P. always regarded it as clearly providential, and without doubt his opinion was correct.

The following entries in his diary, the earliest that have been preserved, will now be intelligible and interesting:

MURFREESBORO, N. C., July 29th, 1841.—To-day my health is quite feeble and I have some very arduous duties to discharge. It is the day of my examination. * * * At nine o'clock the bell was rung, and at ten the exercises commenced. House filled to overflowing. All acquitted themselves with much credit. Afternoon—congregation still larger. Finished our examination and closed with declamation and dialogues, amid the applause of all present. Thus ended the first year of my teaching—thus ended my toils. But that which pleased me most was, that I had given satisfaction to those who had patronized my school.

FRIDAY, 30TH.—To-day I have rest and the pleasure of the company of my sister L. Commenced making arrangements for going up the country.

31ST.—Attended meeting at Parker's with Bro. Thompson. Two received for baptism. Remarks made in behalf of the BIBLICAL RECORDER.

AUGUST 1ST.—Attended Sabbath School for the last time this season, perhaps forever. Attended preaching.

3RD.—This morning bade my dear sister an affectionate farewell. Felt deeply affected. 'Tis hard to part from those whom we dearly love. At 2 o'clock I left M. for Boykin's Depot.

5TH.—Reached the College. Health improved.

6TH.—Spent the day in visiting my old friends—families and students. Much pleased and refreshed.

15th.—In Raleigh. Endeavored to preach in the Baptist Church in the forenoon and afternoon, also to colored people.

22d at Hillsboro. Much fatigued—quite unwell. Attended the Episcopal and Presbyterian churches.

23d.—Feel much better. Oh, that I could feel more thankful. Lord help me more fully to appreciate all thy blessings.

25th.—Spent the day principally in reading Scott's letters. Very interesting. Borrowed Hall's works.—Read his sermon on the death of the Princess Charlotte. Beyond my praise.

27th.—Felt better this morning. After preaching at night in the Methodist church from Mark, 1:15, left Hillsboro for Milton. On arriving at brother N. J. Palmer's, was kindly received by Mrs. P., his good lady. Felt that I was with a friend and endeavored to return my thanks to God for his protecting care, in giving me journeying mercies and placing me among *friends*. O that I could feel and act as God's goodness, long-suffering and unbounded love justly require of me! Lord, help me by thy grace and the influences of thy Holy Spirit to dedicate myself unreservedly to thy service—to do thy will and enjoy thy smile.

28th.—Feel quite feeble after my ride. Took a short walk in the town. Looked at all I saw as a stranger and sojourner, as I really am and as all my fathers were.—Unwell in the evening. Retired early, with thoughts of home and friends far away.

29th.—Endeavord to preach for the people in the Methodist church, from, "Lay up for yourselves treasures in Heaven &c. &c." A large and attentive congregation. In the afternoon went to hear Mr. H. (Presbyterian) preach the first time in Milton.

30th.—Spent the day visiting. Took tea with Sister——. Passed the time conversing on several religious subjects and listening to music sweet enough to charm and captivate the hardest heart.

1st.—Weather beautiful. Health somewhat improving. Rode with brother P. in the country to visit Mrs. Y., a Baptist. At night preached at the

Methodist church. Text, "If any man will come after me, let him deny himself, &c."

Sept. 31st.—My health is certainly improving. Brother P. and I. dined with Dr. G. I was much pleased with my visit.

2nd.—Went to Yanceyville, a delightful village. Everything has the appearance of wealth, refinement and taste. Stayed with brother J. G—. Preached at night in the Baptist church. Text, "What must I do to be saved?"

3d.—Left Yanceyville; went to Gilead and preached. Text, "The men of Ninevah shall rise, &c., &c." Some seriousness appeared in the congregation. I was glad I went to Gilead. Promised to preach there again on the 17th. Returned to Milton.

4th.—Rested to be prepared to preach on Sabbath.

5th.—Morning bright. Health better. Brother P. and I went, on horseback, to Sandy Creek M. H., Pittsylvania, Co., Va.

It appears that this ride to Sandy Creek was his first visit to Virginia. Here commenced a train of influences which was beneficially to affect the cause of Christ in the Old Dominion. God was thus leading him into a field where a rich harvest of souls was to be gathered, to the honor of Jesus. He thus continues his reference to the visit to Sandy Creek:

"Ascertaining that the ordinance of baptism was to be administered, we went to the spot, and saw a man and his companion follow their Lord and Master, 'down into the water,' and 'come up straightway out of the water.' A large concourse of people present. Nearly all strangers. From the water we went to the church, where I preached from 2 Cor. v: 20, 21, to a very attentive and serious audience. Brother Plunkett followed. Text, "Mary hath chosen that good part, &c." Became acquainted with several precious brethren. We then went to Danville. The bell soon rang and we went to church, where I preached from Luke, 18: 1, to a very attentive congregation. Returned much fatigued.
6th.—Morning beautiful. Returned thanks to God, and prayed for the continuance of his blessings both temporal and spiritual. Made several

calls and was earnestly solicited by all to stay and preach that night; but we had to bid them adieu. Ah! this is the lot of all here. We meet but to part. Well, it is right, and we will not complain. But these friends shall all have a place in my memory; yes, always."

Literally were those words fulfilled. The mutual attachment commenced during this visit continued through his life, and his memory is green in the hearts of the people of this section. He thus continues his diary:

"Returned to Milton quite fatigued. I am far away from '*home*,' but I thank the Lord he has given me friends, wherever my lot has been cast. Am exceedingly anxious to hear from home. Hope I shall soon receive letters.

11th.—Arose early to attend meeting at Kentuck, Pittsylvania Co., Va., 12 miles distant. Preached from Gal. II: 20. Some indications of a work of grace.

12th.—Went to church, where we found a large congregation, which the house could not hold. I preached from Heb. IV: 16 and a more attentive assembly I never saw. They crowded the doors and windows. A collection was taken in my behalf. Many thanks to them. I went home with brother W., of Danville, and saw brother Kerr for the first time. Preached at night. 'If any man will come after me,' &c., &c.

13th.—Went to brother Kerr's and spent the day most agreeably with brother Kerr and his wife, an amiable pair. Earnestly solicited by brother Kerr to come and settle in this region and preach, with an assurance of having plenty to do, and being well sustained."

Here the journal is interrupted and we find no more from his pen till after his settlement in Danville, where he was invited to preach Nov., 1841, and was ordained, March, 1842. At this time he became pastor of the church.

In September, 1842, Mr. P. was united in marriage to Miss Mary B. Hinton, daughter of Jas. Hinton, of Wake county, N.C. This devotedly pious lady was indeed a help meet to him and a blessing to the community in which she lived.

For some time, both before and after his marriage, he boarded in the family of Rev. John Kerr, who had been one of the instruments of inducing his settlement in Danville, and for whom he ever entertained a profound respect and a strong affection. He often acknowledged his indebtedness to this aged minister for many valuable lessons.

Until the death of Mrs P., her two youngest sisters, left orphans at an early age, were members of the family and were always regarded and treated by Mr. P. as his daughters. The tender solicitude of their sister and her husband was rewarded in their early conversion. The elder of the two was baptized by Mr. P. in Danville, when but fifteen years of age.

Mr. P's labors while in Danville were very arduous. Preaching at points widely separated, he necessarily spent much time in journeying on horseback to his different churches, and, being very generally known, he was frequently called on to officiate at funerals and weddings and to attend protracted meetings in the surrounding counties. He here commenced what he continued through life, the distribution of religious books and periodicals. He was in every sense of the word a colporteur before that office was recognized in the religious world. The bills containing long lists of books purchased and sold or distributed by him, found among his papers, show the amount of labor he performed in this way.

His influence and usefulness steadily increased, and the last year of his residence in Danville was marked by a most gracious and extensive revival of religion. Not confined to the Baptist church it embraced all denominations and the union and christian fellowship existing during the six weeks of its continuance will never be forgotten by any who were present. Many were added to the various churches in town who have proved valuable members and who still live in various places, bearing evidence to the faithful instructions of this minister of Jesus.

In 1842 he commenced preaching at Bethany, a few miles from Danville. In September, 1843, he held a protracted meeting at that place which resulted in the conversion of more than one hundred persons and in the organization of a church which remains to this day. A gentleman who was one of the first fruits of this revival and who has been an able and useful minister of the New Testament for many years, says: "I well remember the first Sabbath of the meeting. There was a vast concourse of people in attendance. The body of the house, the aisles, the doors, the windows, and every point from which the preacher's voice could be heard, were crowded and still many were unable to gain admittance or to hear. After the services were opened, a hoary-headed but irreligious man, pressing through the crowd, begged in behalf of the congregation that the preacher would occupy a stand near the door, exclaiming with evident emotion, 'Mr. P., we want to hear the Gospel.' The request was granted, and as Mr. P. arose to address the people he remarked that such a hungering and thirsting after the glorious gospel of the blessed God filled his soul with an overwhelming sense of the Divine presence, and but for the hope that his humble efforts would be blessed to the good of souls he could say with Simeon of old, 'Lord, now lettest thou thy servant depart in peace, for mine eyes have seen thy salvation.' The audience was melted to tears and many dated their first serious convictions from the services of that hour. At the close of the meeting a church was organized with a membership of more than fifty, from which number God called two young men to the work of the gospel ministry. Similar results attended his labors with the other churches in this region."

In the minutes of the Roanoke Association for 1844, we find the following:

"*Resolved,* That Elder John L. Prichard be requested to explain the objects of the General Association and make a collection in aid of its funds to-morrow."

"Lord's day. Elder Prichard commenced the services of the day with a sermon from Isaiah 53: 5. Elder James followed with a discourse from 2 Cor. 4: 1-2, after which Elder P. explained the objects of the General Association and took up a collection amounting to $20.20."

Again, in 1845, "Rev. J. L. Prichard laid the claims of benevolent societies of Virginia before the Association and took up a collection amounting to $23.83."

These are the first instances in which specific reference is made to raising funds for benevolent purposes in this Association. The following extract from the writer already quoted will enable the reader to understand them and appreciate their importance. He says, "While Mr. Prichard's labors here were greatly blessed in the conviction and conversion of sinners, his special mission has ever seemed to me to have been another, which if not so pleasant was scarcely less important. Differences of opinion had divided the old Roanoke Association into the Dan River and Roanoke Associations, the former incorporating in her constitution the obligation resting upon the churches to aid in sending the gospel to the heathen; the latter denying this obligation, though some of the leading brethren and a few of the churches acknowledged it. The honor of revolutionizing this important and influential Association, the Roanoke, was conferred on J. L. Prichard. At the first session of the body which he attended he introduced resolutions in favor of Foreign Missions. They were voted down. He then announced that he would present the claims of the enterprise and take up a collection on the Sabbath. The Association objected. He replied that he would not in any way compromise the body, but it was his duty as well as his inalienable right to do whatever he could to extend the Redeemer's kingdom among men, and this right he should exercise wherever his lot might be cast. On the Sabbath, therefore, he eloquently presented the claims of Foreign Missions and then took up a collection, himself going among the congregation to receive their contributions. Many who have since cast their hundreds into the treasury of the Lord, that day gave their first dime. The effect was wonderful. Public opinion was rapidly revolutionized, and at subsequent sessions of the body the resolutions which are given above were unanimously adopted."

The following account of the same matter is from the pen of Rev. A. M. Poindexter, D. D.:

"As a member of the Roanoke Association, he at once took a decided stand in favor of the cause of missions. The Association had long been disturbed and crippled by Antinomianism. To escape the unpleasantness and injury resulting from this, twelve churches in 1840 asked for letters of dismission, and formed the Dan River Association. The withdrawal of these churches did not bring peace to the Roanoke Association. The Antinomians had represented those who withdrew, as the cause of all disturbances. But no sooner had these withdrawn, than they determined to force from the position of neutrality, into their own course, the remaining churches. Failing in this they withdrew and formed the Staunton River Association—a decidedly Antinomian body. This second division with concurring events, tended to prepare the Association for the reception of liberal views. This result was accelerated by the labors of Rev. J. J. James, who for a time preached stately at Strait Stone, and perhaps elsewhere within the Association; and of Rev. Elias Dodson, who, as a missionary of the General Association, sustained by the Dan River Association, travelled regularly and extensively among the churches; and the occasional labors of others. But at the commencement of brother

Prichard's connection with the Association, the results of these labors were but little seen. He at once decided upon an independent course. The Association met at Republican Grove in the spring of 1842. On Lord's day he addressed the assembly on behalf of missions, stating that he did so on his own responsibility, and should give to any who might wish to do so, an opporutnity to contribute. After an earnest appeal he requested brethren to pass through the congregation and receive contributions. It was done, and the exercises were productive of much good feeling. This course he pursued at each session of the Association until the fall of 1844. Then, thinking opposition sufficiently overcome, he stated, in the session on Sunday, that he had enjoyed the honor of these collections as long as he desired, and now wished to transfer it to the Association, and proposed that they order a collection to be taken next day. It was agreed to, and from that time the Roanoke Association has ranked as a missionary body, and has become to a considerable extent liberal."

It will thus be seen how potent for good was his influence in this ancient body of believers. It required strong love for the cause of missions, and a strong will to breast the current of opposition which had set in against it. Many of the opposers were greatly his seniors, and were held in christian regard on account of their labors in the ministry. But he believed them to be mistaken, and a solemn sense of duty to the heathen, and to the Author of the great commission, urged him on.

What renders this action more worthy of note is the fact, that the Association was thus led back to the practical acknowledgment of a principle which had been dear to the able men who were active in its earlier history. John Williams, one of the fathers of the Roanoke Association, referring to the spread of the gospel in Virginia, about the period of the Revolution, thus expresses himself: "May the Divine effusion become general, and the blessed Jesus go forth conquering and to conquer, until his name and his praise be one in all the earth." John Weatherford, also a minister of this body, and who in 1773 was for weeks in prison as a preacher of the gospel, evinced the same spirit. When Judson went to Burma his heart was greatly elated, and as he learned the story of his labors and sufferings, he expressed the liveliest concern for his success. It was the privilege of Mr. Prichard to become the instrument of bringing back the Association to the recognition of that claim which looks to the spread of the gospel in heathen, lands and which had been opposed or ignored.

A few extracts from letters written by him during the period already referred to, will not be uninteresting.

NOVEMBER, 2nd, 1841.

"*My health has not been so good for five years. How thankful I feel for this. I had a very pleasant time in Fayetteville. I remained until Sabbath evening and preached every day to a large, attentive and serious congregation. Many were made to cry, , What shall I do to be saved?' Two professed hope in Christ and I have no doubt there were others. To day I leave Hillsboro for Milton. I am exceedingly anxious to get home. No place so sweet as home.*"

DANVILLE, Dec. 24th, 1841.

"*My health has been unusually good. I am as pleasantly situated as I could wish. I receive the kindest attentions from all classes. There is a most excellent feeling existing among all the different churches at this place. I am as often invited to the houses of Presbyterians and Methodists, as by the Baptist brethren, and as often go.*"

DANVILLE, May 9th, 1842.

"*My health since I saw you has been unusually good. I feel quite confident that a few years in this healthy and delightful region will entirely restore my health. For this I feel humbly thankful. My mind has recently been greatly exercised in consequence of a call I received while in Raleigh to come and take the pastoral charge of that long neglected church. For what cause I cannot tell, my brethren generally and the church unanimously urge me to come to R. They seem to think I could succeed in building up a church in that place. But I fear they are mistaken in this. I have been much at a loss to know how to decide. I have endeavored to make it a subject of prayerful consideration to ascertain. 'Lord what wilt thou have me to do?' After calm, deliberate consideration, I have thought it best to remain where I am, at least this year, or until circumstances shall seem to indicate more plainly that I ought to go. I dislike the idea of appearing fickle and unstable, being well aware that much of a man's success in life depends upon his strict integrity and firmness of principle.*

It is a high compliment paid to a man, when it can be said of him in truth, 'He is a man to be relied upon; what he promises, he will most assuredly perform.' This is the character I have long been endeavoring to form. How well I have succeeded I leave for others to judge. There are many things that I could name, which have induced me to remain here. This is certainly, by far the most healthy region of country. It is also a more productive and plentiful region. Here too is a wide and inviting field of usefulness. I know of no position of ministerial labor, that promises a richer harvest of precious souls to a faithful minister of Jesus Christ, than that in which I am now engaged. 'The fields are white already to harvest.' And the cry comes from many more places than I can possibly attend, 'Come and help us;' 'Will you come and preach for us?' I preach every Sunday to large and attentive congregations. My brethren in Va. say that they cannot consent for me to leave them. They offer me many inducements to stay and co-operate with them.

"I am not sure that I shall not attend the General Association of the Baptists of Va., to be held in the city of Richmond on the 1st Sabbath in June. I have just returned from an Association held in Halifax Co., Va., where we had a most pleasant meeting and where I greatly enlarged the circle of my acquaintance. I am solicited to preach at Halifax C. H. Probably I shall do so."

DANVILLE, June 8th, 1842.

"I received your deeply affecting letter on the 19th. I cannot say I was surprised at the sad intelligence of the death of your affectionate father. Though I did sincerely hope that he might again recover and be restored to the bosom of his dear family, yet I knew that nothing but Divine interposition could bring that to pass. I feel that I can sympathize with you and your dear mother, because I know by sad experience what it is to lose a tender and affectionate father. It brings afresh to mind the grief that wrung my young heart, and the tears that so freely flowed when I saw one of the best of fathers laid in the cold and silent grave. It affords me consolation to hear you express your resignation to the dispensation of that Allwise and good Being. 'He doth not afflict willingly.' With all my heart I adopt your prayer, that 'it may prove a blessing to each of our souls.'

The following extracts speak of his attendance on the General Association of Virginia, from whose meetings he was rarely absent.

(TO HIS WIFE.)

JUNE 4th, 1843.

"*We arrived in Richmond about 4 P. M.; stopped at the Columbian Hotel, where a great many persons, not less than one hundred, I judge, sat down at once. We went to the Herald office, then walked about some, and at night attended a concert of sacred music at the Second Baptist church. The music was delightful, soul-enrapturing. They had several instruments, but none so sweet as the human voice.*

Friday morning the Bible Society met in the Second Church. We had a delightful meeting, several very good addresses, full of thrilling interest. At night attended preaching. We were invited to Brother Crane's and are now with him. He has a very pleasant family. Brother Stringfellow is staying there with us and others.

Saturday morning the General Association convened. There is a large attendance. I do not know the number. Sabbath was a delightful day. I attended Sabbath School, was delighted. In the morning heard Andrew Broadus preach—in the afternoon, A. McClay, of New York. At night, Burrows, of Philadelphia. Most of the pulpits of the city were filled by Baptists. I have never seen anything to equal the splendor of the First and Second Baptist churches. They were filled with attentive hearers. The music was heavenly.

I do not regret my trip. I have formed many acquaintances. Am much pleased with the Richmond people; they are kind, plain and hospitable. There is among them, I think, much deep-toned piety. I have been mostly over the city. There are many splendid edifices, the "Exchange" particularly. There is much here to please the eye, delight the ear, and affect the heart for good and for evil. There are many warring elements. Truth and error, vice and virtue, wordly mindedness and heavenly mindedness, each striving for the mastery. God grant it to virtue, piety and godliness. I wish some of our Danville friends could come here, and see that they are not the only folks in the world. To-day we meet again; shall adjourn Wednesday, I think not before. My health was never better."

The next meeting of the Association is thus referred to:

RICHMOND, JUNE 2d, 1844.

"*We arrived at this "many-hilled city," about six A. M., Friday.
Are staying at Brother Wortham's, and as comfortably lodged as we could
be. At 11, A. M., Friday our anniversaries commenced. The American and
Foreign Bible Society met at the First Church. A great many delegates had
arrived. We had an interesting meeting. I did not attend church at night,
having travelled all the night before. Saturday the General Association
met. Brother Hume, of Portsmouth, preached at 11, A. M., an excellent
discourse on 'The want of spirituality in the church.' Evening session—
very interesting. A committee being appointed to say where the next
meeting of this body should be held, Lynchburg, Richmond and Petersburg
were proposed. On this question several speeches were made. The
question being taken, it was decided by a large majority that it should be
held in Lynchburg. Brother Walker, of Hampton, preached the Education
sermon last night—very good. This morning at 9 o'clock, I heard Brother
Bagby preach at the Penitentiary.*

*I cannot describe my feelings when I saw before me more than one
hundred convicts from 18 to 40 years old, and this was only half of them—
only half being allowed to come out at a time. The sight was enough to
make one's heart sicken within him. At 11 o'clock, to-day, I had the
unspeakable pleasure of hearing Andrew Broadus. This afternoon, did not
attend church. There has been much good preaching here to-day. Dr.
Babcock, from New York, is here, and also brother Harrison, of New York.
I have to preach to-night in the Methodist church. I trust the Lord will help
me to preach, to His glory.*

*There are a great many persons in the city at this time, and much
to interest, please and profit. I was quite unwell the first day and a half,
but now I feel very well indeed; how could I feel otherwise when I see such
a host of able ministers of the New Testament?*"

A letter is here inserted, written during his attendance on the
General Association in 1846, and indicating the special pleasure he
enjoyed in meeting the missionary from China, and his native assistant:

RICHMOND, JUNE 6, 1846.

"*MY DEAR WIFE:—I have delayed writing until this morning because I wished first to be settled. My ride on the first day and night was quite fatiguing. I travelled all night, but had the entire stage to myself, and my overcoat for a pillow, and could have slept quite comfortably but for the rough road. I reached Henderson at seven the next morning, where I rested until five in the afternoon, and felt quite refreshed and prepared for another night's travel. We passed through Petersburg at five in the morning and reached Richmond at seven, having travelled all night. I went to the Columbian Hotel to breakfast, rested awhile and walked up to Ball & Harold's, where I met brother Jeter, who took me home with him. I am very agreeably situated with brethren W. H. Jordan, A. M. Poindexter and D. Witt. Sister Jeter is fast sinking with consumption. How mysterious are the ways of Providence! I think she is fully ripe for Heaven.*

Our meeting commenced yesterday. There seems to be a full delegation and brethren are still coming in. At this early hour many from a distance are here to attend the Southern Baptist Convention. Brother Shuck and Young Seen-Sang are here. I took tea with them last night at brother T's. Brother Shuck is quite a young looking man. Young Seen-Sang delivered an address last evening, interpreted by brother Shuck. He is a singular but noble looking man. His dress is a loose robe, coming just below his knees, under which are loose trowsers. The forepart of his head appears to be shaven; but behind, his hair is suffered to grow and is plaited in a cue, nearly four feet long. He is of a bright mulatto color, and wears a cap.

I have much to attend to and shall have to close, but shall write again soon. Nothing is wanting now to make me perfectly contented but the presence of my two Marys. How is the dear little one? Kiss her many times for papa. Love to mother, sister and the little girls, and servants, and accept a double portion from your affectionate husband."

The following letter was addressed to a relative who had just entered the ministry:

DANVILLE, VA., MARCH 3D, 1847.

"*MY DEAR BROTHER L:—I trust the apology my wife has made for our long delay in writing is entirely satisfactory. The place which I have bought was so much out of repair that I found it necessary to work, myself, very hard, and now my hands are in no condition to write. You will remember the place, when I tell you that it is at 'Lover's Leap,' where you and I walked. I hope soon to make it a very desirable residence.*

My dear brother, I am truly glad that you have devoted yourself to the office of the christian ministry. There are some few things I may take the liberty of suggesting to you. There will be not a little expected from you by the churches and your family. Many eyes are turned towards you, as one who is to be eminently useful. But especially the cause of Christ has claims upon you superior to all others. And in order to meet these expectations and these claims, it will be necessary to have a fixedness of purpose. 'Give thyself wholly to these things,' always esteeming the approbation of Christ and your own conscience, as being worth far more than all things else. My sincere prayer for you is, that you may be an able minister of the New Testament, a 'burning and a shining light,' that many may rejoice in your light, that God may give many seals to your ministry as stars in your crown of rejoicing, and that at last you may say, 'Lord, here am I and the children thou hast given me.'

Sincerely and affectionately yours,

J. L. PRICHARD."

The "new residence" to which reference is made in the above letter, was situated on an eminence commanding a fine view of Danville, from which it was separated by the Dan River. Here he resided for about four years, during which time the place was much improved by his labor. The bridge over the Dan River having been carried away by a freshet in August, '50, and his residence being thus isolated from the scene of his pastoral labors, a circuitous and rough ride being necessary to reach Danville, he removed into the town—feeling, also, that his time could be more devoted to his great work when not interrupted by attention to a farm.

PETERSBURG, JUNE 6TH, 1848.

   "MY DEAR WIFE:— * * * * * *I have now been absent a week, and a long one indeed it has seemed. I had a pleasant trip, and reached Petersburg early Thursday morning. I have been staying at Mr. D.'s His family has indeed been very kind. We have had a very interesting meeting. I have met many acquaintances. And now the meetings are all over and we have given each other the parting hand. All are in a great hurry to get home. I confess I have no little struggle in my mind to decide what I shall do. I want to be at home with my dear wife and sweet little babes—names full of music to me. Kiss my dear little Mary and Robert many times for me. Give my love to Eugenia and Fannie, and the servants. I expect to start for Norfolk in the morning—shall make but a short stay in Camden.*
   * * * * * * *And now, dear wife, let us pray that God will bless us all, and permit us once again to meet, more determined to consecrate ourselves to the great work of spreading the Redeemer's kingdom.* * * * * * *"*

   As may be seen from the foregoing letters, he was always present at the meetings of the General Association of Virginia, enjoying the exercises much. He was equally regular in his attendance at the Southern Baptist Convention, not permitting slight obstacles to prevent it. In April, 1849, he started to the Convention, which had been appointed at Nashville, Tennessee, but on account of the appearance of cholera in that section, the time and place of meeting was changed. The following letters refer to his disappointment, and his perseverance in accomplishing the object for which he set out:

WILMINGTON, APRIL 25TH, 1849.

   "MY DEAR WIFE:—How strange are the ways of Providence! How little do we know of what is before us. The future to us is a blank which every moment is filling. And how differently it is filled up oftentimes from what we expect. You see from the date of my letter that I am now in Wilmington, N. C. You can scarcely imagine my disappointment when at Goldsboro I met the cars from Richmond, to find that not one of the brethren from that place was in the cars. Disappointed and discouraged I

scarcely knew what to do. I determined, however, to go on, and on reaching Wilmington, I came very near going on board the steamer and being off to Charleston. I thought, however, I would go and see brother McDaniel. From him I learned that the Convention would not be held in Nashville, but in Charleston on the 23d of May. So I am now within twelve hours sail of the Convention. Brother McD. invited me to stay with him and hold a protracted meeting. I have concluded to do so. I shall be absent until the last of May. The trip will not cost me a fourth of what it otherwise would. I expect to be all the time engaged in preaching. I trust that this decision will meet with your approbation, and that of my brethren. * * * * * * * * *"

WILMINGTON, May 8th, 1849.

"MY DEAR WIFE:—* * * My mind has been greatly relieved, to hear of the goodness of the Lord to you, our dear little ones, and all the family. Blessed be his holy name! It is a great comfort to me, to have you so cheerfully acquiesce in what seems to be a Providential arrangement. Especially as I feel, in your own language, 'to be acting in the conscientious discharge of duty.' I assure you that nothing else could induce me to forego the pleasures of my family. No place on earth is to me like home. No pleasures like those I find in the bosom of my family.

Brother Tompkins is dead! O my soul, be thou quickened on thy journey, live thou nearer to thy God, and be thou more conscientious and faithful in the discharge of all thy duties! I feel that I have lost a brother and a friend.* * * * * * * * *Wilmington is a much larger place than I expected; over eight thousand inhabitants. It has much commercial importance. You can have no idea of the quantity of lumber, tar, turpentine, &c., that find a market here. Shipping, from various parts of the world, may be seen. I went on board of a ship from Liverpool and have seen several others from Europe. In every direction, you see turpentine distilleries, steam, saw and grist mills, rice mills, &c.

I have preached several times since I have been here, and expect to preach to night, and many more times. Time moves slowly. It seems that I have been absent a long time. But it will soon fly off, if I can only be usefully employed. We expect to start to Charleston, Monday week."

CHARLESTON, May 24th, 1849.

"MY DEAR WIFE:—The Convention met yesterday, about eighty delegates present and more expected. The business is nearly laid out, so that we are now at work. We were most cordially received. This is a beautiful and fashionable city. * * * * I shall expect to leave here Tuesday and go directly home. May God, in his mercy, keep you all in safety and may we soon be permitted to see each other and then I can tell you all about things I have seen and heard. * * * * *"

Having been so long absent from home, he failed this year, for the first and only time, to attend the meeting of the Association, which occurred soon after his return.

CHAPTER IV.

A SEVERE TRIAL—SICKNESS AND DEATH OF HIS WIFE—
LETTERS REFERRING TO THIS EVENT—ATTENDANCE UPON
GENERAL ASSOCIATION—VARIOUS LETTERS—SECOND
MARRIAGE—CALL TO LYNCHBURG—YANCEYVILLE
MEETING—REMOVAL—ESTIMATE OF HIS WORTH AND
LABORS.

In the midst of abundant labors, the subject of this memoir was called upon to suffer a severe calamity in the death of the principal member of his family. Perhaps no man was ever more happy in the ties which bound him to the home circle. In the selection of a companion for life, he seemed to have been directed by his all-wise, all-gracious, Heavenly Father, and he had cherished the hope of many years of unbroken domestic felicity. His wife and children he loved with an ardor never exceeded. In the joys of his happy home he found an unspeakable delight. Often, as he returned from his long, wearisome journeys, to attend his appointments, he realized a peculiar refreshment and comfort in the presence of his family. Unbending himself from the severest duties of his ministry, he evinced a tenderness and affection of manner which showed how pure and deep was the current of his domestic bliss.

But it was the will of God to arrest this tide of earthly joy. His much loved wife gave early indications of declining health. She suffered much from general debility for many months, and then premonitions of decay were beheld by him with deepest grief. No earthly affliction could have been apprehended, so painful as a separation by death. But his divine Sovereign, the same gracious Friend that gave her to him, was about to visit upon him this affliction and to take her away. This was to be a part of the discipline requisite to a better preparation for the great work before him. He was to be himself a sufferer, that he might know how to sympathise with and comfort the sorrowing.

Mrs. Prichard's health had declined so much in the summer of 1849, that a trip to the Virginia Springs was recommended. It was tried, apparently with good effect. She seemed to rally for a while, but soon after her return she began to decline again, and it was evident that the end was approaching. On the 24th of November she was removed from her sphere of usefulness on earth to her home of glory in heaven, leaving two children, a son and a daughter, who still survive. An extract from the Danville *Register* shows the estimation in which this excellent lady was held by the community in which she lived and died:

"The deceased was, in the true sense of these terms, a kind friend, an obliging neighbor, a faithful mistress, a dutiful child, a fond mother, a devoted wife, a true christian.

This excellent lady came among us, a few years since, a *stranger,* with no relative or *even acquaintance* to welcome her arrival. By a meek and humble life, in short, by an exhibition of every christian grace and a practice of every christian virtue, she so won the confidence and affection of this whole community, that when the church bell tolled her departure, sorrow and sadness seemed to fill every heart.

As the solemn procession passed through our streets, and during the services at the church, the doors of the stores and work-shops were closed, their occupants uniting with every portion of our population in honoring the memory of one whom all acknowledged to be one of 'the most excellent on earth.' Truly may it be said that this was a striking exhibition of that involuntary homage which mankind, even in its fallen condition, feels constrained to offer to exalted virtue.

"Let no one speak of her as dead. 'She is not dead, but sleepeth.' Fitter for Heaven than Earth, she has been removed to her appropriate sphere, where she lives and will forever live, in immortal health."

The closing scenes, and the views and feelings of Mr. P. under this afflicting dispensation are best given by himself:

(TO HIS BROTHER-IN-LAW.)

DANVILLE, NOV. 19TH, 1849.

"DEAR BROTHER L.:—I have no doubt you wish to be informed of the condition of your sister. None but those who are constantly with her can have an idea of what she suffers at times. And yet in the midst of her sufferings she is enabled to rejoice in Christ Jesus. This morning after reading to her the language of Paul in Phillippians, 'That I may be found in Him, not having mine own righteousness which is of the law, but that which is through the faith of Christ, &c.,' she exclaimed: 'O husband, what a precious thought it is, to be clothed in the righteousness of Christ; had I a thousand lives I would devote them all to His service. I never felt him more precious in my life.' * * * Her appetite is not good, and to this I attribute the more rapid decline of her strength. We do not know how long she has to suffer thus. We can only say with Job, 'Have pity upon us, have pity upon us, O ye my friends, for the hand of the Lord God hath touched us!' My dear wife sends much love to you all. The rest of the family are well. Pray for us my brother that we may be sustained. We feel the need of your prayers.

Sincerely and affectionately

Your brother,

J. L. PRICHARD."

(TO THE SAME.)

DANVILLE, NOV. 25TH, 1849.

"*MY DEAR BROTHER L.:—With feelings unutterable I sit down to communicate to you the mournful intelligence of the death of my dear wife. She died on Saturday evening, twenty minutes before 6 o'clock, with the consolations of that blessed religion that had sustained her in all her protracted and painful illness. No one could have borne such suffering with more fortitude and resignation. She retained her senses to the very last, spoke to me not more than two minutes before she breathed her last. I have not now time to write particulars of her illness and death. Bro. Wait preached her funeral to-day in the Baptist Church, and she was interred in the public Burying Ground. It was her special request that brother Wait should preach her funeral before she was buried, if she should die while he was at Yanceyville, and that she should be buried where she is. Greater demonstrations of sympathy for us, and of sincere affection for her, could not have been shown. All the stores in town were closed, and I believe nearly all the community attended her funeral. I feel, my dear brother, that I have lost my best earthly friend. We are smitten in the dust, but we shall see her again.*

> '*Yet again we hope to meet her*
> *Where no farewell tear is shed.*'

O, I do wish you all could have been here with us. We did not expect she would die so soon. Dr. G. thought she would live two or three months or more. But the blessed Saviour came at an hour when we did not expect Him. She longed to be gone, and I doubt not she is now with all our pious relations in Heaven. Pray for us and believe me

Your sincere brother,

J. L. PRICHARD."

These extracts evince the deep feeling of grief endured in this painful trial, and the power of christian principle in sustaining the sufferer.

God was his support. He found at this period a peculiar comfort in committing himself and his motherless children into the hands of the Lord. Nor did he intermit his labors in the ministry. He seems with new energy to have fulfilled his pastoral duties, and to have preached the word with more than usual earnestness and power.

His engagements at this time were numerons and pressing. Besides a large congregation, and a church which had become flourishing under his care in Danville, he filled a monthly appointment at Harmony Church, and another at Bethany, both in Pittsylvania county. At all these points he labored with increased fidelity, and was favored with tokens of the special blessing of God.

About this time, too, he was greatly encouraged in seeing several young men, some of whom were baptized by him, enter the work of the gospel ministry. He in this recognized the special favor of the great Head of the church, for he had been praying and waiting for some to be raised up in that region, who should become pleaders for Christ. In the letter which follows, he refers to the joy he experienced in connection with these results. Writing to a christian friend he says:

DANVILLE, JULY 24TH, 1850.

"I have been constantly engaged since returning from the General Association. I have baptized four persons since I saw you, and expect to baptize one, next Sabbath, who was a soldier in the Mexican war, and now wishes to become 'a soldier of the cross.' I trust he will 'endure hardness as a good soldier of Jesus Christ,' and fight manfully the battles of the Lord. We commenced a protracted meeting on the evening of the 18th, which is still in progress. We have had a crowded house. Several of my young brethren in the ministry have been with me and preached with great acceptance to our people. This, to me, is inexpressibly gratifying. I have stood here almost alone for nearly nine years, and have had but little assistance in this way. I trust, however, that my labors, imperfect as they are, have not been in vain in the Lord. One of these young brethren I baptized. He is now tutor in Wake Forest college, and a young man of great promise. Another of these young brethren was recently ordained pastor of the church in Milton, N. C. He bids fair to be a very useful man and an acceptable preacher. There is a young brother Ferguson, who preached in the afternoon of last Sabbath to our people, who took us by

surprise. He has only been licensed five or six months, and I feel that his discourse would have been listened to with interest in your highly favored city. He is now teaching school, but will go to college this winter. I am deeply interested in these things. * * * * * * * * * * * * * * * There is a most excellent state of feeling existing here between the different churches. At eight in the morning we agree to pray at home, and at four we meet at the church, and at night we have preaching. At these times, 'though sundered far,' may we not feel that by prayer 'we meet around one common mercy seat?"

(TO THE SAME.)

AUGUST 17th, 1850.

"Our meeting though pleasant, was not so profitable as we fondly hoped it would be. Good, I have no doubt, was done. There was much seriousness and our congregations were constantly large. We expect to renew our efforts soon. My time is very precious now. Our Association meets next Friday, over sixty miles from here. I shall have to leave here on Wednesday, as I am appointed to preach the introductory sermon."

About the same time, in a letter, he refers to his attendance at the meeting of the Association, when very decided measures were adopted, bearing upon the work of missions. He seems especially to rejoice in this. He thus writes:

"I left home on Wednesday, after I wrote you, to attend our Association, and the next day reached Whiteville, within four miles of the church at which our meeting was to be held. My route lay through a most interesting portion of country, not far from Dan River at any point. The fields of corn were indeed beautiful. The fruit trees were bending and even breaking, so full were they of the most delicious fruit. I felt that this was truly a land that the Lord had blessed, 'a land of corn and wine and oil, favored with God's peculiar smile, with every blessing, blessed.'

"On Friday morning, I reached the church, through quite a heavy shower of rain. Soon most of the delegates assembled, and I preached the introductory sermon from Acts XVII: 16. The Association was then called to order, and letters from twenty-three churches were read; I was chosen

Moderator, and the usual business was attended to. Several corresponding messengers and visiting brethren were present—Mason, Shaver, Gwaltmey, Jennett and others. The attendance was large. Our session was truly a harmonious one; I have never attended one so pleasant. I feel that our body may now be called, truly, a missionary body. A systematic plan of benevolent effort was unanimously adopted. I think we shall carry it out. Efficient ministers, under the blessing of God, is all that we need. We have the numbers and the ability. My visit was a most delightful one:

"On Saturday night we had a storm of wind and rain such as has not been seen, for many years. The water-courses were all full. Nearly all the bridges on Staunton, Banister and Dan Rivers are gone. Our bridge at Danville is gone. The crops are greatly injured, if not destroyed. Thousands and tens of thousands of dollars will not repair the losses.

"On Thursday reached home, found all well, and felt truly thankful that my crops had suffered but little. Early Saturday morning, I left home for my appointment at 'Harmony church,' fourteen miles west from Danville. This is my appointment for the first Sabbath in the month. Next Sabbath is my time at 'Bethany church' six miles north east of Danville. On the third and fourth Sabbaths I preach in Danville.

"Every sympathy of my heart has been drawn out for your father and the family. If the 'fervent prayers' of God's people can 'avail' anything, then I feel there is good reason to hope for the speedy recovery of one loved by all.

"I feel that I know something of your present feelings. I know them, because I have been schooled in them. I can truly say, 'I am the man that hath seen affliction.' When I was but ten years old, I was called up from my bed, at midnight, to see my father die! It is all fresh in my mind now. The anguish that wrung my youthful heart cannot be forgotten. My mother was thus left a widow, with six children—the oldest but twelve years old, two sons and four daughters, and, alas! two of these 'are not.' In 1845, I visited 'my native land,' Camden county, N. C. Then we were all alive. We parted to meet no more 'till Gabriel's trump shall sound.' Since then two of my sisters, both mothers, have died. They were lovely sisters. Both of them were truly pious. My mother has lived to see all of her children members of the church, and in this we have been wonderfully blessed. Though she is now sixty-five years of age, I know of no person of her age, more active, cheerful and happy. You see, without proceeding any farther, that I have passed through scenes of affliction.

"One thought in connection with affliction is consoling. It is that we have to endure the same affliction but once. Every one borne, leaves one the less to bear. Every wave moves the frail bark nearer the shore. How different do afflictions seem to us whilst we are passing through them, from what they do after they are gone. Now we are as the fearful mariner, upon whom is coming the terrible storm with its angry billows. Look which way we will, all is danger! We surely shall be swallowed up! 'Hath God forgotten to be gracious? Is his mercy clean gone forever?' 'Be not afraid, 'tis I,' is the voice that hushes every murmur of the winds, calms every wave, lights up the countenance, and thrills the heart with joy. And now, that same storm, that was our terror, having passed us, is an object truly sublime and beautiful—God's 'bow of promise' is between us and that, assuring us that, 'behind a frowning providence, he hides a smiling face.' Other storms of afflictions may come; but this one, never. It is gone, gone forever.

"I trust I can say, 'It is good for me, that I have been afflicted.' You say, you fear you know nothing of that change of heart, which you have professed. Is this the first time, you ever had any misgivings on this subject? In this, I can assure you, you are not alone. Of all the afflictions of this life, there is none like the hidings of God's face.

> 'There's not a drop of real joy,
> Without thy presence, Lord.'

"I have much bitter experience in this too. I trust I can say to you, as was said to me by Brother Wait, President of Wake Forest College, when I was in great distress of mind, as to my 'acceptance in the Beloved.' 'God,' said he, 'is preparing you for a great work. How could you comfort the distressed, if you had never tasted the bitter cup?' Feel assured you have my sympathies and prayers.

"My last Sabbath was indeed a pleasant one and, I trust, profitable also. Brother Hankins was with me. We both preached. The congregation was large, attentive and serious. We expect to commence a protracted meeting there (Bethany) on the 29th. I feel there is some interest in our congregations. O for a general outpouring of the Spirit upon us all! This is a lovely evening. The sun is fast sinking. The prospect from my window is beautiful. It commands a view of several miles of undulating surface. The *last rays of the sun are tinging the distant hills and the tree-tops. And now, 'our spirits meet,' in prayer, 'around a blood bought mercy seat.' "*

The following communication gives some insight into the feelings of the christian minister, in view of the responsibilities and privileges belonging to his office.

DANVILLE, Sep. 24th, 1850.

"* * * * I spent the third Sabbath in this month, in the pleasant little town of Milton, N. C., with my excellent brother Lacy. I preached several times to his congregation and trust that good was done. I returned home on Tuesday, found all well, and was made to feel as none but a father can feel, when met by my sweet little Mary and Robert. I have given them to the Lord. I wish to 'train' them for Him. The weather during the past week has been delightful. Being busily engaged in my preparations for the Sabbath, the week glided almost imperceptibly away. Our meeting on Saturday was pleasant. Most of the members were present, though many of them live in the country. My family remained in town all night. I went home and spent that beautiful moonlight night a one. And yet, I felt, I was 'not alone.' With my books, and singing and prayer, 'I forgot all time, all care and pain.' 'I laid me down and slept; I awaked for the Lord sustained me.' O! how beautiful and bright was that Sabbath morn! 'Safely through another week, &c.' expressed the sentiment of many a glad heart on that lovely morning. I went early to the Sabbath School. And what an interesting sight was there. About sixty scholars were present. All seemed delighted. At eleven, I preached to a large and deeply interested congregation from I Peter, 1: 4. I felt it to be a great privilege to preach such truths to God's people. They seemed to enjoy it. After sermon, we assembled around the 'Lord's table,' and there partook of the bread and wine and I think there were many who felt to ask,

'Why was I made to hear thy voice? &c.'

"In the afternoon I held a meeting for our colored members. We have about one hunded. We restored one, heard them sing some of their sweet songs, &c.

"At night, I preached again to a densely crowded house, on the training of children, having often been requested to do so. It is a subject about which I have thought and read much. I know of nothing more important or in which I take a deeper interest. * * *"

His tender sympathy for the afflicted is evinced in the following lines:

DANVILLE, Aug. 17th, 1850.

"* * * Most sincerely do I sympathize with you in the affliction of your dear father. I am gratified to hear you express yourself as you do, in reference to this severe trial. 'Godliness is profitable unto all things.' You must not expect to feel an entire acquiescence in his dealings with you at first. It requires much prayer and meditation and exercise of faith. Jacob, with all his piety and experience, was unprepared to part with Joseph and Benjamin. 'All these things are against me,' said he. But when he saw through the whole he said, 'It is enough.' David was grieved when he saw 'the prosperity of the wicked,' but when saw their 'end,' then he ceased to envy them and complain against God. Paul was impatient under his affliction, whatever it was, until God assured him, that his 'grace should be sufficient for him.' And then, but not till then, he most gladly acquiesced in God's will. So it must be with us. The christian life is a growth. We should have great reason to suspect ourselves, if these trials and afflictions did not, to some extent, render us unhappy. Disease, whether moral or physical, struggles hard and long against the remedy. And during this struggle the patient must of necessity suffer in body or mind. But, though painful at present, 'twill cease before long. And then how pleasant the conqueror's song."

(TO THE SAME.)

"Earth has no sorrow that Heaven cannot cure."

"Yes, in despite of all that sin has done for our world, there is much of happiness to be enjoyed here after all. 'The bitter is sweet and the medicine is food.'

"What could we do in many of the conditions of life without the consolations of religion? And yet sustained by these consolations, the very trials, afflictions, anxieties and disappointments of this life, are converted into so many wings and pleasant gales, to lift our souls above, and waft us to some Pisgah's top, from which we have a view of the heavenly canaan. And, O, what a view it is! What foretastes! I rejoice to know you derive such comfort from the 'precious promises' with which our Heavenly Father's word is filled."

October 30th, 1850, he was married to Miss Jane E., daughter of Rev. Jas. B. Taylor, D.D., of Richmond, Va. In this, as in his former union, he was peculiarly favored. Mrs. P. proved a mother to his little children, so sorely bereaved, and to himself a wife in the highest sense of the word—a help-meet in all his labors, and a comfort in his trials.

He remained in Danville, preaching there and in the adjacent country, ten years—busy, fruitful years as we have seen. A flourishing church organized at Bethany; two hundred and fifty six members added to the church in Danville, and all his other churches greatly revived and strengthened under his ministry; the Roanoke Association saved from antinomianism mainly through his instrumentality;—these are some of the fruits with which his earlier labors were crowned—enough for a life-time surely. But his stay here was drawing to a close. He was strongly attached to the people of his charge and tenderly they loved him in return. But his life had been one of unceasing activity and arduous labor, and he longed for a place in which he could have more time for study and self-improvement. Nor was he long in finding it. In January, 1852, he received a unanimous call to the church at Lynchburg, and soon afterwards removed to that city. With this statement we resume our extracts from his letters and diary.

The accompanying letter was addressed to his wife from Yanceyville, whither he had gone to fill his regular appointment. For some time he had been serving the church at this place in a monthly visit. His connection with this people had been peculiarly pleasant, and the happiest results had attended his ministry. The interest which existed in the congregation at this time, is referred to:

(TO HIS WIFE.)

YANCEYVILLE, NOV 25th, 1851.

"*I am now alone in an upper-room, comfortably seated by a good fire, and my thoughts turn to you and my dear little ones at home. You will be glad to know how it has been with me and what are the prospects for a revival, &c. I reached here in good time, preached to the church, had a pleasant meeting. The church agreed unanimously to invite brother Reynoldson to come and hold a meeting. On Sabbath morning I preached to a very large congregation, had prayer meeting at 3 o'clock, and preached again at night—congregation good, attentive and serious. Monday I spent in visiting from house to house. The day passed off pleasantly. Christians seem anxious for a revival. Held prayer meeting at, 4 P. M. I preached at night; seriousness still more apparent. I feel encouraged to go on. I believe the Lord will bless us. I received a letter this morning from brother Reynoldson. He expects to be here on Friday, so I do not see how I can come home this week. Eighty persons had professed in Milton up to yesterday, and twenty one are now anxious—a great and glorious work is going on there. I sincerely trust we shall have a good time—I know I have your prayers that I may be faithful and successful.*"

(TO THE SAME.)

YANCEYVILLE, DEC. 4th, 1851.

"* * * * *I wish to keep you informed of the state of things here. Tuesday night we had a good meeting. Several professed and many more became anxious. The congregations have been large and attentive all the time. Last night we had the best meeting of the series. It was a solemn time. The people seemed loth to leave the place. They lingered, they wept, they rejoiced. Up to this time thirty have professed, and there are now over twenty inquirers.*

"*I feel it to be my duty to stay here now, and I therefore think I shall not go to Harmony. I trust you will agree with me in believing it my duty to remain here. It seems that this is the time to thrust in the sickle and reap, 'for the fields are already white unto harvest.'*

"Friday morning—A beautiful morning. I had a pleasant night's rest and hope to be able to do something to-day to glorify Him who suffered for us. I trust I am making sacrifices for Christ in thus leaving 'wife and children, &c.,' even though it be but for a time. God knows my heart, and I can appeal unto him, that it is no little sacrifice to be absent so much from those who are so dear to me. But this is the time to suffer and make sacrifices, and the only time. For in that blessed world above, our employment will doubtless be of a different kind. You, too, are no less making sacrifices. There is a cross for every one, and there shall be for all a crown. You will remember that they who staid and took care of the stuff, shared equally with those who went out and fought the battles. Yes, eternity will declare it that she who remained at home in quiet, and, it may be, unknown to the world, has done much of the work. She is hid from the public view, pouring oil upon the flames that opposition and discouragement would extinguish.

"Love to all. Kiss the dear children many times for papa and believe me ever your affectionate husband."

The meeting to which the above letter refers resulted in the conversion of a number of persons, some of whom, it will be seen from succeeding entries in his journal, he baptized on the day he dissolved his connection with the church.

EXTRACTS FROM HIS DIARY.

"Jan. 8th 1852.—Received a unanimous call to the church in Lynchburg.

10th.—Saturday. Bethany meeting. Did not go. It snowed until dinner. Spent the day mostly at home. Talked much of the probability of going to Lynchburg.

11th.—Still cold. Ground covered with snow. Went to Bethany. Met only a few, with whom I read the scriptures, sung, prayed, and talked some.

12th.—Spent the day resting. Mind much engaged. What shall I do? Shall I go? or shall I not go? Lord, direct.

17th.—A solemn day. Formally resigned the care of the church in Danville, having held it ten years. There was much deep feeling by us all. None blamed.

18th.—Rained all day. Preached to a small congregation. Had some liberty in speaking. Trust some good was accomplished.

19th.—Intensely cold. Wrote a letter of acceptance to the Lynchburg church. Brother Palmer spent the night at our house—the coldest recollected by any of us.

20th.—The coldest weather ever known here. The falls entirely frozen over. Ice from 5 to 6 inches thick. Began to make arrangements for moving."

To decide upon a course was, with him, to act, as will be seen by his rapid preparations to enter upon his new field of labor.

"21st.—Still extremely cold. Mercury below zero. Could do nothing except keep good fires.

23rd.—A little milder. Went to brother H's., on my way to Yanceyville. Spent a pleasant night, much religious conversation.

24th.—Yanceyville. Made two calls and then met a good number at church. Received fifteen by experience. Resigned my charge. A very solemn time.

25th.—Sunday. A beautiful morning. Very large congregation. In the afternoon baptized fifteen. An immense crowd present. Preached again at night and took leave. Much feeling by us all."

He was compelled to visit Lynchburg to make arrangements for removing his family and was absent four days.

"Feb. 1st.—Sunday. Danville. Preached to a large congregation. Took a review of the ten years' labors, I trust with good effect. Much sympathy manifested for me and my family.

2nd.—Commenced packing with brother M's. help. Many friends called in. We loaded the wagons before night and my family went to brother W's.

3rd.—Transacted much business. Paid off accounts. Visited and took leave of only a few families.

4th.—Made an early start for Lynchburg, travelling till sun-down, and stopping through the night at Mrs. B's.

5th.—Started at sun-rise. Mild, pleasant day. Reached Mr. Hollins' house in Lynchburg about sun-down. Devoutly thankful to God for his mercy."

The retirement of Mr. Prichard from a field which he had so diligently cultivated for a series of years, was the result of a stern conviction of duty. As already stated, he desired the opportunity of devoting a larger portion of time to systematic theological reading. In leaving Danville, however, he found himself the subject of painful emotions. He had scarcely known how strongly attached were the people of that whole region, to him as their spiritual counsellor. He had been abundant in labors in the county of Pittsylvania, and in the surrounding counties, and in every direction the seals of his ministry were to be found. The sincerest grief was manifested by many, that they were to see his face no more, in the regular assemblages where they had been accustomed to meet him. It is not strange that when the parting hour came, he should have felt deeply under the pressure of fraternal love so strongly evinced.

The estimate in which he was held in Danville and its vicinity is revealed in the following tribute furnished by a highly intelligent gentleman of another denomination:

"Although I was not a member of his congregation, it was my privilege to be on terms of intimacy with Mr. Prichard, and to be a frequent attendant on his ministry. I have had, therefore, a good opportunity of observing his manner of life, and of judging of his ministerial fidelity and efficiency.

"His preaching was plain, direct and pungent. He never addressed the imagination or endeavored to *please the fancy* of his audience. He had too correct an appreciation of the solemn nature of his calling to lower the dignity of the christian minister by seeking to attract the admiration of his hearers to *himself.* His effort was rather to induce them to fall in love with, and heartily receive the great and *important truths* which he was commissioned to proclaim.

"As a pastor he labored zealously to instruct the ignorant, to reclaim the wayward, to reform those who had gone far out of the way, and to confirm and comfort such as habitually strove to continue in the right path. He rebuked with firmness yet with affection, exhorted with earnestness, and reproved with a fearlessness which was characteristic of himself.

"He had the courage to discharge his duty, under circumstances which would have discouraged if not appalled most men. His, however, was not the brute recklessness of danger which distinguishes the lion of the forest, but that true *christian courage* which was founded on the assurance that whilst he was in the path of duty, he was surrounded and shielded by an Omnipotence which was pledged for his protection and on which he could confidently trust for safety and deliverance. With this conviction he went forth to the discharge of duty, nor felt nor feared the danger that beset him. The only fear he knew was that he should 'come short of the promise set before him;' or, as St. Paul expresses it, that 'after having preached the Gospel to others' he himself should be a castaway.

"I have often remarked that I had never known an individual on whom I would more confidently rely, to march up to the cannon's mouth, if duty should call him to the trial. This was the estimate which was put upon his character by all, in this region of country, who had the pleasure of knowing him.

"That such a man should exert a wide and a healthy influence in the church, of which he was an ornament, might have been reasonably expected. And so he did. It was mainly through his instrumentality that the anti-missionary spirit, which at the time of his coming among us was in the Association to which he attached himself, was crushed out and this body became an active co-worker with those who were endeavoring to obey the great command, 'Preach the Gospel to every creature.' Nor was his influence confined to his own church; his presence was a strong though silent rebuke to all evil-doers wherever found."

CHAPTER V.

DESCRIPTION OF LYNCHBURG—ENTRANCE UPON THE NEW
PASTORATE—DISCOURAGEMENTS—DIVERSIFIED LABORS—
COMPLETION OF MEETING-HOUSE—DIFFICULTIES IN THE
CHURCH — ADJUSTMENT — MRS. HOLLINS—TEMPERANCE
CAUSE—INCIDENT—LETTERS—RESULTS OF LABORS IN
LYNCHBURG—CALL TO WILMINGTON—ACCEPTANCE—
LABORS IN LYNCHBURG.

Lynchburg is the most important place in that section of Virginia lying between the head of tide-water and the Blue Ridge, and known as the Piedmont country. It contains about ten thousand inhabitants and derives its importance from being the junction of the Orange & Alexandria, the Southside, and the Virginia and Tennessee railroads, and till recently the terminus of the James River and Kanawha canal; from its position as the centre of trade to a fertile and extensive region; and from its numerous and large manufactories. The great staple of tobacco, specially, here finds a mart second only to Richmond, while its manufacture is conducted on a scale which gives the place a national, if not a world-wide reputation. One of the features which most struck the stranger, walking through the streets in former years, was the sonorous swell of song which constantly rolled from the busy, cheerful negro laborers engaged in the various operations by which the weed is prepared for the use of the consumer.

The city is romantically, if not pleasantly situated on the hills which rise precipitously from the waters of the James, and is in full view of the Blue Ridge just distant enough to wear that azure hue which most enchants the soul of any one who has an eye for the beautiful in nature; while the far-famed Peaks of Otter, towering like Alps on Alps constantly direct the mind from the busy, changeful scenes of life to thoughts of the infinite and the everlasting.

The steepness and roughness of the streets must, however, largely absorb the attention of the pedestrian in Lynchburg, or he is likely to be in the condition of the philosopher of old, who, wrapt in the contemplation of the heavens, stumbled over the milk-pail placed in his path by a mischievous maid. We remember on one occasion, visiting Lynchburg, we were directed by a friend to his residence somewhat thus: "Keep up the street, and go any way you can without breaking your neck and you will not go wrong." We thought, at the moment, the direction exaggerated, but when we pursued the course indicated, seeing on one hand frowning cliffs, and on the other yawning ravines, we felt that it was not so. Even the principal thoroughfares of the city, paved though they are, still retain a grade which renders them almost impassable when covered with ice, and a weariness to the flesh of the pedestrian on a summer day, while the stone steps constantly occurring give ample warning that vehicles may not pass, nor even horsemen unless they be of nerve which would make them worthy to follow a Forrest or an Ashby.

To the pastorate of the Baptist Church in this place, Mr. Prichard was called in January, 1852, and after mature deliberation decided to accept the position. To this conclusion he was led, not by a desire for change, for no man ever had less love of novelty; not by anxiety for a larger or more pleasant field, for the one afforded by a residence in Danville could scarcely be surpassed; certainly not from any alienation between himself and the churches which he served, for the mutual confidence and love increased rather than diminished to the close of the connection. We believe that the one motive which decided him to remove to Lynchburg was, that confining his labors to a single church and relieved from the necessity of spending a large portion of time on horseback, he might enjoy at once the stimulus and the opportunity for reading and elaborate preparation for the pulpit.

But the care of the Lynchburg church by no means afforded a position for the enjoyment of quiet, literary leisure. On the contrary, probably no church in Virginia, of its size, demanded a greater amount of exhausting pastoral labor. We remember to have heard Dr. Ryland say in a public address that when he was pastor in Lynchburg, the property of the church, leaving out a single member, did not average a good cow for each family. Under the labors of Smith, Clopton, Shaver and Williams, it had indeed increased in ability; but still the majority of the members were poor and were scattered over the hilly suburbs. The church had been without a pastor for more than a year before Mr. P's. settlement among them, and the congregation had in consequence been dispersed. During the pastorate of his predecessor, Rev. J. W. M. Williams, now of Baltimore, a new building had been commenced and had progressed sufficiently for the basement to be used as a place of worship. But after Mr. W's. resignation and removal, the church became involved in a lawsuit with the contractors and the enterprise was suspended.

Here then was the first work of the new pastor. It was to gather the scattered flock together and win their confidence and affection; seek out and restore the congregation; and finish the house of worship. It was an herculean undertaking, and yet he did not falter or shrink from it. As nothing could be done on the house till the lawsuit was decided, he devoted himself the more assiduously to the exploration of his new field. Some conception of his spirit and his labors at this time may be gathered from the following entries in his diary:

"**LYNCHBURG, Feb. 7th.**—Saw many of the brethren, who appeared to be in fine spirits. Felt encouraged. There seems to be much harmony of feeling. I have no language to express our gratitude for the goodness which has attended us.

8th.—Pleasant morning at Sabbath School. Talked a little to the children. Preached to a good congregation.

March 4th.—This day moved *home*. Feel thankful that we are once more at *home*. O that it may be home to us in the Lord! God preside over us, and rule in us, and guide us!

5th.—Much engaged in fitting up and arranging for the comfort of my family; find it fatiguing, having all the errands to go myself.

6th.—During the past month could do little, except in getting ready for my regular pastoral duties.

21st.—Spent the day in preparation for Sabbath. Felt it was good to be alone with God and my books.

APRIL 1st.—Still in my study, writing my sermon. Feel it a great privilege thus to be permitted to study God's Holy Word and prepare for more extensive usefulness.

14th.—Preparing a sermon on *justification*. Am deeply interested in my subject. Company came in. Could not do much. Need much patience.

15th.—Hard at work on my sermon. Had a quiet day. O, how delightful to study the Scriptures. Enjoyed the day."

25th. Sabbath. Attended Sabbath school. Preached in the morning, Sunday school sermon, to a large and attentive congregation. At night from Col. I: 28. Much good, I trust, done.

29th.—In my study, reading the life of Lord Bacon, as reviewed by Macaulay. Much interested, and more surprised than interested.

MAY 2nd. At Sunday school—a good number present. Preached on 'Justification,' and again at night on the 'Blessings of Justification.' Had quite a good time."

The diary for this year here ends. The diary for 1853 is continued but a few months, and the entries are simply to refresh his memory as to the events of his daily life as they pass. Many are such as this:

"Spent to-day visiting the following families, &c., &c."

"This day passed off pleasantly in my study, &c."

Such was the pressure upon his time, amid his diversified duties, that little opportunity was left even to make a record in his journal. Over the hills and in the suburbs of the city he was constantly engaged in visiting the families of his flock, while a due attention was given to the preparation of his sermons. The hours appropriated to reading and study were peculiarly prized, and when on any account they were lost to him, it was felt to be a real affliction. In a constant endeavor to enlarge his range of general knowledge, and especially his acquaintance with theological truth, his library became an object of peculiar interest. He rapidly improved in his investigations of the word of God, and in his method of sermonising. His profiting was thus made to appear to all. It was soon found that the basement-room of the house of worship in which the church met, was beginning to be inconveniently small. The congregation had been increasing from his first entrance upon the pastorate. He now turned his attention to the removal of the difficulty which the law suit involved, with the purpose of securing the completion of the upper room. It was due to his discreet management of the whole matter that it reached a speedy issue.

The lawsuit, to which we have referred, being decided, the only barrier to the completion of the house of worship, now rendered a necessity by the constantly increasing size of the congregation, was the lack of funds. Pastor and church zealously and heartily co-operating, the requisite amount was secured in a few days, and after a season of patient waiting the work was done. The event is thus recorded in his diary:

"Preached from Isaiah LIV: 23, 'Enlarge the place of thy tent, &c.' Gave notice that our new house of worship, would be dedicated next Sabbath.

7th.—Went to my house to prepare a dedication sermon, but brethren coming in to have some conversation, did no writing."

The above is explained by the fact that interruptions in his study, which was in the basement of the church, were so frequent that he retired for greater privacy to his own dwelling.

8th.—"At home at work on my sermon. The ladies putting down carpet in the church. I spent the day pleasantly, reading and writing.

9th.—Still at work on my sermon. Have become deeply interested in the subject. Hope I have learned something.

10th.—Sermon nearly completed. Spent a part of the day at the church, altering some doors.

11th.—At home nearly all day. Finished my sermon and feel greatly relieved. Willing now to have Sunday come, and yet feel much anxiety.

12th.—The day fine for finishing our preparations. Purchased materials for cushions and aided in completing the arrangements.

13th.—Dedication. Dense fog in the morning. Cleared away and sun shone out. A large congregation. Preached from 1st Tim. III: 15. Communion at 3 o'clock, and preaching at night from Phil. II: 14, 16.

14th.—Beautiful day, which I spent in visiting. Delightful church-meeting at night."

After the above date his diary was intermitted and not resumed till 1856, from which time it is continued till the day he was stricken with the fatal disease. One more entry is found which will suggest something of his manner and influence with his servants:

"APRIL 8th, 1853.—This morning, at 9 o'clock, Dick died of pneumonia, after a sickness of over four weeks. We feel this to be a great affliction. Well, I did all I could. The will of the Lord be done. We shall miss him much. He was a faithful servant, and I sincerely believe a christian. I had some interesting conversation with him a few days ago, last Sabbath especially. O, let us try to do our duty and be ready."

During Mr. P's. pastorate in Lynchburg some difficulties in the administration of church discipline arose, which for a time impaired his usefulness and put to the test all his wisdom and firmness. In these trials he manifested those traits of character which marked his course through life, mingled tenderness and firmness. His family and the brethren and sisters who stood by his side in the season of painful perplexity can testify to the sleepless nights and anxious days through which he passed. But he steadfastly maintained his position, and the cloud ere long passed away, and he rejoiced in the thought that matters were settled, as he believed, finally, and that the members of the church could unite their energies and efforts to promote the Redeemer's cause among men. In the following extract from a letter to a friend he tells the story of his trials:

LYNCHBURG, April, 22nd 1853.

"*DEAR BROTHER L.—Since I last wrote you, I can almost adopt Ps. LII: 7. 'All thy waves and thy billows are gone over me.' Almost, I say, not fully, 'deep hath called unto deep,' but in the midst of the roaring of the storm, I heard a voice saying, 'Be not afraid; it is I' and still another, 'it is through much tribulation, we must enter the kingdom of heaven' and 'these are they that have come out of great tribulation, &c.' Now don't be alarmed—but to the point. We have had great difficulties in the church, difficulties of thirty years standing. They did not commence during my ministration. You recollect your first visit to this city, the first time you gazed with rapturous delight upon the Blue Ridge! You know that I was going to Lynchburg to assist in settling a difficulty in the church. A committee of about sixteen of our experienced brethren, ministers and laymen, labored from Wednesday until Saturday, day and night, and hoped we had adjusted the difficulty. But some of the 'old leaven' was left, and has been at work ever since. I very soon saw it was impossible to build up a church of the materials then in it—endeavored to act cautiously and discreetly, and to take no step without much deliberation and prayer. We excommunicated one, and about a dozen have taken letters. We have now about one hundred and forty members, and a more united, working set of men and women I have never seen. I think it likely the minority will form another church. I hope they will and go to work. So, it may be, we shall see the proverb fulfilled, 'There is that scattereth and yet increaseth.' God grant it. I rejoice that He can make the wrath of man to praise Him. I do not judge these brethren. I can but hope they mean to do right. But I certainly think they have greatly erred.*"

In the above extract a reference is made to the cordial co-operation of the members of his church in all his plans and labors. Perhaps no pastor was more happy in this respect. In the adjustment of the long pending difficulty, the church seemed to enter with new energy upon the work of building up and extending the cause of truth. Several notable examples of efficiency in this work might be named. One of these examples especially deserves attention in this memoir. From the earliest history of the church, Mrs. Ann Hollins had been one of the most consistent and useful members. Her husband, Mr. John Hollins, an enterprising and successful merchant of Lynchburg, though not himself a member of the church, spared no expense or pains to gratify his wife in all that related to the building up of the Baptist cause. She was indeed and in truth, a helper in the Lord. Singularly gifted as she was, in all that ennobles the sex, she consecrated herself and her talents to the promotion of her Redeemer's glory. For several years she was the principal support of the Baptist interest in Lynchburg. Nothing could divert her from the cherished purpose of her heart, to live and labor for its promotion. When the Baptists were few, poor and despised, she clung the more closely to [illegible text] [illegible text] appropriations were large and liberal. Every object of christian benevolence shared in her benefactions.

The large and flourishing Female College at Botetourt Springs received from her an endowment of several thousand dollars, and its name was changed as a tribute of respect to Hollins Institute. In all these deeds of love, her excellent husband evinced an abiding sympathy. Both of this noble pair have passed away. It may be said of them, "Lovely and pleasant in their lives, and in their death they were not divided." Those most intimately acquainted with Mr. Hollins rejoiced in the assurance that he died an humble believer in the Lord Jesus, and that he with his much loved companion now swells the song of redemption in the bright world above.

In Mrs. Hollins the subject of this memoir found a personal friend and earnest co-worker, and carried with him to the end of life a grateful estimate of her sympathy and influence.

In Lynchburg, as at all times and in all places, Mr. Prichard was the zealous advocate of Temperance. During the earlier part of his ministry in that city, an effort was made to elect only such municipal officers as were in favor of restricting the issue of licenses to sell intoxicating liquors. Of course the movement excited active and bitter opposition. In the progress of the struggle an incident occurred which is in every way honorable to

Mr. P. We give it in the words of the friend who has kindly furnished it for publication:

"The prospect, to the friends of Temperance, had become very dark. Its enemies were about to triumph. The best talents, legal and other, that they possessed were brought into requisition. Plans laid in secret were about maturing. A panic seemed to seize even those who had been pillars in the cause. But a few hours and the meeting would be held and the final blow would be struck. Late in the day Mr. P. was informed of the state of affairs. His mind was made up. His friends feared for him, not that they doubted his ability but lest his well known excitability should carry him too far. Some of the friends of Temperance urged the abandonment of the cause. Others, embarrassed, knew not what to advise. The prevalent impression was, that inaction was the highest policy. At the appointed hour a dense throng filled the hall. The Commonwealth's Attorney who had been looked to, as a champion, by the friends of the cause, but had declined to speak on the ground of its uselessness, united with others in urging Mr. Prichard to decline also, for his own sake and that of the cause. He replied, 'I'll speak if it's the last time I ever appear before a public audience; if it costs me my life I'll speak.'

"A Judge and a prominent lawyer appeared in favor of the traffic and delivered able addresses. It was then time for Mr. Prichard to reply. Never was he known to be more calm, more self-possessed. Point by point, with the accuracy of a practiced pleader, he took up and answered the arguments of his opponents, exposing and shattering their gilded but hollow sophistries. He seemed to revel amid the creations of his own fertile fancy. The audience was so thrilled and electrified by the powerful, burning portrayals, that, at a word from the almost inspired speaker, they would have turned on his opponents and thrust them from the hall. Said a gentleman who was present, 'I have heard eloquence on other occasions, but nothing I ever heard has enabled me to realize, to such an extent, what is said of the overpowering force of Patrick Henry.'

Some who had been cool towards him on the ground of religious denominationalism, took him to their arms from this time, and to the latest hour of his sojourn in this city manifested the genuiness of their conversion."

His letters, which are given below, are descriptive of his life in Lynchburg, and tell what needs to be told better than we can do it. During a temporary absence of his wife from home he thus writes:

*"Last Sabbath was a delightful day. At seven in the morning I baptized Mrs. N.; a precious season. We had a good Sunday School, a large and attentive congregation. Subject, 'Ye shall know the truth and the truth shall make you free.' John VIII: 32. It was communion season. Again at night, a good congregation. I have visited several families this week. * * * You know something of my trials and discouragements here. But you do not know all. I feel that I need all the consolation that this world can afford me. And I do know that there is nothing in this world that can contribute so largely to my consolation and encouragement as your sympathy. Till we meet let us often remember each other at a throne of grace, that God will bless us and our children and make us a great blessing to the people among whom our lot is cast."*

(TO THE SAME.)

JULY 12th, 1852.

" * * * * Yesterday was a very warm day, but very good congregations, and I felt more than usual, I trust, while endeavoring to discharge my duty to them. In the morning my subject was, 'And Moses, when he was come to years, refused to be called, &c., &c.' At night, 'I was alive without the law once, &c.' I trust a good impression was made. I felt much exhausted when I reached home. I am very feeble this morning and shall not visit as usual to-day, but remain at home and rest."*

(TO THE SAME.)

LYNCHBURG, March 28th, 1853.

" * * To day I had truly a pleasant time in my study. Really enjoyed my work. Finished my preparation for Sunday—wrote, for a rarity, several letters and then took a little recreation. Last Sabbath our congregation was good and attentive—subject: 'Wilt thou not revive us again? &c., &c.' In the afternoon I went to hear Rev. Mr. Mitchell, but it*

*was communion. Quite a goodly number out and they had a solemn time. I preached at night from the words, 'Men, brethren, and fathers, to you is the word of this salvation sent.' I think there was some tenderness in the congregation. Thank you for your words of encouragement—I need it. By the help of the Lord my mind is made up. I offer myself a sacrifice to his cause here. * * *"*

(TO THE SAME.]

LYNCHBURG, April, 4th 1853.

" * * Many thanks for your promptness in writing. I feel thankful to our kind Preserver that you have been 'kept by a Father's eye,' and that the dear little boy, though sick, has also been mercifully preserved. Ought we not to be devoutly grateful that our children have had and recovered from most of the diseases common to childhood? Many parents have had to part with their dear little ones, whilst ours are spared to comfort us. O that it may be to comfort us, and prove a blessing to our race! I do want us to feel that our children are the Lord's. Let it be our constant prayer that God will, at an early age, change their hearts. We have much to encourage us in doing this. His word abounds with encouragements, and in your own family you have a practical demonstration of these two truths—God's faithfulness and the parent's reward. * * * * * * * * My time has been occupied as usual. I spent the entire day on Tuesday in visiting. Wednesday and Thursday I was closely engaged with my books and papers. Wednesday night a large Temperance meeting was held at Temperance Hall. Mr. Edwards and I addressed the meeting. It was by far the largest meeting that has been held for a long time. It was the anniversary of the Lynchburg Division. * * * * *"*

(TO THE SAME.)

LYNCHBURG, April 11th, 1853.

" * * * I would have liked you to peep in just about the time I was seated to read your letter. Grandma stopped her knitting, Sister her work, and M. and B. their play; and all were intent on hearing it except little B., who could not refrain from an occasional glance at his pretty new book.*

*All of us were delighted at the references to ourselves. Expressions of love from absent friends are, beyond expression, sweet. The christian is surely not in want of proofs of God's love when he looks back upon a life crowned with loving kindness and tender mercies, but notwithstanding all this, such is his nature, he often wants a renewal of these same tokens. Moses had seen and enjoyed much of the loving kindness of the Lord, yet his prayer was, 'I beseech thee, shew me thy glory.' And Philip's desires were increased by what he had seen, to ask, 'Lord show us the Father and it sufficeth us.' Now the application of all this is easy and natural. The fields that were refreshed by the showers in days past, will soon need the return of the clouds again. Often have you contributed to our happiness and most heartily do we thank you for a renewal of these proofs. You are in the midst of those who love you tenderly, but feel assured, there are none in R. who think of you oftener or more affectionately than does one little group in L. Your absence and dear little Jemmie's has created a void, that nothing but your return can fill. * * * * * * * *Our congregations on Sabbath were very good and attentive. Many of the Episcopalians were out, as they had no preaching at their church. To-night is our church meeting. I trust we shall have a pleasant time. It is now getting to be a rare thing to have our former difficulties spoken of. We are determined to let the matter die. I think the citizens care but little about it. * * * * * The church in Liberty will be dedicated next Sabbath. I have a pressing invitation from the church and pastor to attend. Shall probably go on Saturday."*

(TO THE SAME.)

APRIL 18TH, 1853.

"Another week with its responsibilities, anxieties and privileges has gone to vast eternity since I last wrote you. So I am another week nearer to my journey's end and to my dear ones whom I long to see. I do love to think of that one idea of heaven, given us in Revelation: 'And there was no sea there.' No, there is nothing there to separate us from those we love. Here, 'lands and rivers roll between, &c.' Well, it can all be turned to good account. It will only make heaven the sweeter. Self-denial is no small part of religion. And I will look at Christ, think of Him, and 'press towards the mark, &c.' You will wish to know how I have passed my time. On

Tuesday and Wednesday I was in my study. Monday night we had church-meeting. It was a very pleasant one. Two joined by letter. Others will join soon. Thursday, at 10, I preached the funeral of Mr. E. at our church. He was buried by the Odd Fellows. Text: 'O death, where is thy sting, &c.' Friday morning was beautiful; I spent the day in visiting. Saturday, at six o'clock, I took the cars for Liberty, and reached there at seven. It commenced raining about eight and continued all day, much of the time very hard. So I preached the first sermon in the new church—text: 'One thing have I desired of the Lord, that will I seek after, &c.' I enjoyed it much and I believe the congregation more. It was off hand completely— the number of people out was small, as it rained. I was interested in my subject—intend preparing a sermon from that text some of these days. I reached home a little after five, having enjoyed my trip much. Brother C. L. Cocke came to Liberty as I left. I had little time to speak to him. He is anxious I should attend the examination of the school at Botetourt Springs, in May, and make an address on education. He has made me a life-member of the Virginia University Education Society.

Yesterday was rainy—Sunday School small. I preached to quite a good congregation—text: 'I will guide thee with mine eye, &c.' I spent the afternoon profitably I trust, reading Bishop Butler's sermons on the 'Son of God,' and 'Self-deceit.' I would recommend them to every christian. He goes to the bottom of things, analyzes them, tests them. I preached to a small congregation at night in the basement. I went down, not expecting to preach, and did not carry my sermon, but preached from the words of the Publican."

* * * * * * * *

(TO THE SAME.)

LYNCHBURG, MAY 1st, 1855.

"*I left home Thursday, for Franklin, with brother C. and reached Gogginsville at nine that night, having crossed the Blue Ridge twice, through it on the cars and over it on the stage. Gogginsville, though in the midst of the mountains, is east of the Blue Ridge proper. It was warm and very dusty travelling. During the night the wind blew quite hard and the next morning was cool, fire being comfortable. Friday morning we went to church, met a small number of persons, to whom I preached. Then held a consultation with brethren Goggin, Brown, Leftwich and Sanderson in reference to what we should do next day. The next morning, on going to the church, found the house full, examined the individuals, fourteen in number, and organized the church. I then preached, by request—subject: 'Co-operation of church and pastor.' Being much fatigued, I left at intermission but brother Leftwich preached.*

Sunday was a beautiful day and a large congregation was out. The house did not hold all the ladies and many gentlemen stood all the time of my long sermon—text: 'Whom God hath set forth to be a propitiation, &c.' After an intermission brother Goggin preached. I then rode over a beautiful mountain, a distance of six miles, to Rocky Mount, at the earnest solicitation of the people of that place, and preached to them on 'Christ's second coming.' After preaching I laid down on a sofa until eleven o'clock, when I was aroused by the stage-horn.

We left Big Lick at nine and reached Lynchburg at twelve, finding all well at home. I was delighted with Franklin county and think the prospect very encouraging. The General Association must send them a good preacher and I feel sure the people there will very soon take care of him. They more than paid my expenses, and one gentleman said if they would get me to preach once a month he would give $25. I would not be afraid to go there at once without an appointment from the Board. Almost feel like going, felt so much at home there. People so hungry for preaching. 'When will you come again? Do come and see us often,' were remarks frequently made.* * *"

Mr. P's labors in Lynchburg were drawing to a close. They had been arduous and incessant and had been prosecuted, as we have seen, in the face of many discouragements and often of fierce opposition. But nothing daunted, he pressed forward patiently, cheerfully, earnestly, and triumphed in the end. His pastorate in Lynchburg extended through four years and had been eminently successful. The little flock, scattered and almost discouraged, had been gathered together and encouraged and strengthened. Seventy-seven members had been added to the company of believers, thirty-seven by letter and forty by baptism. The neat and commodious house of worship, which at his coming, seemed likely to fail of completion if not to pass out of the hands of the Baptists, was finished, and it stands there to-day to tell of his patient perseverance in well-doing.

The discordant elements in the church had either been harmonized or removed, and a long career of peaceful, useful labor seemed opening before him. His brethren thought that he ought not to entertain the idea of leaving. But, though he loved Virginia as he had reason to do, his heart turned yearningly to his native State, and two invitations received at the same time from different quarters decided him to return. The circumstances attending his removal and the motives which influenced him are best narrated by himself.

EXTRACTS FROM HIS DIARY.

DEC. 21ST, 1855.—"This day received a call to the pastorate of the First Baptist Church, Wilmington, N. C."

As was his custom, he without delay proceeded to make the inquiries necessary to enable him to come to an early decision.

27th.—"Left home to visit Wilmington. Reached there at seven, the next morning, and spent Saturday and Sunday there, preaching twice, and left Monday to return home.

JAN. 2ND, 1856.—Received letters from Trustees and President of Oxford Female College, inviting me to take charge of the same.

3rd.—Had an interview with some of the brethren in reference to the calls to Wilmington and Oxford. What shall I do? Lord, direct in the right way.

4th.—Had conversations with brother M. and sister H. All seem deeply affected and none more than I. *I feel it my duty to go,* but dread to say so to the church. O Lord, send them a better pastor than I have been, and bless him.

5th.—At home all day. Talked much about going to W. Wrote to Oxford, declining the call.

6th.—Sabbath. Beautiful and bright. Preached from Rom. XII: 1, 2. Gave notice of a church-meeting Tuesday night.

7th.—Saw some of the brethren and conversed with them in reference to my leaving. Wrote to W., indicating my acceptance of the call to the pastorate of the church.

8th.—Consulted with some of the brethren about leaving, a successor, &c. At the meeting that night offered my resignation, which was accepted, and the very kindest sentiments of regard for me expressed, and deep feeling evinced by all."

In his letter of resignation he says: *"Most of you are aware that, within the last few weeks, I have received a call to the pastorate of the Front Street Baptist Church, Wilmington, N. C. You are also aware that, in order to enable me to decide more correctly and speedily what I ought to do, I have made the church a short visit. And now, dear breathren and sisters, after much anxious and, as I believe, prayerful deliberation I feel it to be my duty to offer to you my resignation as pastor of this church.*

"Let me assure you that it is no diminution of love to you personally, or to the church and congregation generally, that has influenced me to take this step. So far from this I have never been, nor do I ever expect to be, associated with a people to whom I shall be more attached. I entertain the kindest feelings for every member. Nor can I allow that any one feels a livelier interest in the prosperity of the church than I do. You have been uniformly kind to me, and courteous in all our intercourse, in the church and elsewhere. You have been prompt in meeting your obligations to me and my family. At the end of every year my salary has been paid. To part from such brethren can not but be painful.

"I trust I shall be believed when I say a sense of duty, and this only, has prompted me to sever the connection which has subsisted for nearly four years. I feel that I can be more useful there than I can expect to be here.

"And now, dear brethren and sisters, may the great Head of the church guide you in securing an undershepherd who shall be more able to instruct and comfort you, and more successful in winning souls to Christ, and thus building up a large, efficient and prosperous church."

We continue the extracts from his diary:

9th.—"Much engaged in making arrangements to leave.

11th.—A number of brethren and sisters called. It was a pleasant time.

12th.—Snowed! Snowed! I piled up wood and had coal brought. I do feel devoutly thankful for all my mercies. 'My times are in thy hands.' Lead me, O Lord.

13th.—Beautiful day and much warmer. Preached in the morning in the basement; at night in the upper part to a good congregation. Took a retrospect of my coming here and all that had transpired. It was an affecting season.

14th.—Attended church-meeting at night. Had a most delightful time.

15th.—Packed my books and attended prayer meeting at night. Lectured from John XV. Quite a good number out, and I really enjoyed the meeting. Hope some good was done. O Lord, direct the church.

As in Danville, so in the city he was now about to leave, a general feeling of regret prevailed among all classes of the people that his valuable ministerial services among them were about to close. This feeling was manifested in various ways. The families of his own congregation were ready to yield to a feeling of sadness in sundering the ties which had bound him to them. He had so often knelt with them at the family altar— had been their counsellor and comforter in times of difficulty and trial, and had shared so freely in all their joys, that they felt as if they were about to lose a sincerely cherished friend. Even the children evinced sorrow at his departure. He had always shown the kindest sympathy with them in all their pains and pleasures. The citizens also, and members of other religious congregations shared in this feeling of regret at his removal.

It would seem scarcely in accordance with a wise discretion to change a field of labor under under circumstances such as existed in this care. But as already suggested, from the time of leaving his native State, the most urgent appeals had been made to induce a return. Oxford, Newbern, Raleigh and other positions had been brought before his attention, and flattering inducements to occupy them were repeatedly presented. May it not be believed that in this, as in other events of his history, his steps were ordered by the Lord?

CHAPTER VI.

WILMINGTON, NORTH CAROLINA—PASTORATE
COMMENCED—SENSE OF RESPONSIBILITY—HEAVY LABORS—
ASSOCIATIONAL MEETINGS—SYMPATHY WITH THE
SUFFERING—FAMILY AFFLICTION—DEATH OF A CHILD—
EXTRACTS FROM DIARY AND LETTERS—AFFLICTION
SANCTIFIED—REMARKABLE REVIVAL—EXTRACTS FROM
DIARY AND LETTERS.

Wilmington is pleasantly situated on the east bank of the Cape Fear River, thirty five miles from its mouth, and is the largest town in North Carolina. In 1860 it had a population of 9,500, with a considerable and rapidly increasing trade. It was the principal depot for the exportation of cotton, turpentine, &c. from an extensive and productive region, and here the imports for a large part of the State were brought in.

The first Baptist church in this city, as we have seen, had extended a call to Mr. Prichard and he had accepted it. He reached his new field of labor on the 31st of January, 1856, as appears from the following:

JAN 31st.—"Arrived in Wilmington at 8, P. M. First prayer-meeting there to-night. O, how thankful that we are at our journey's end."

The following entries may be surprising, perhaps amusing, to some who remember Mr. P's. fluency in extemporaneous discourse, but they are characteristic—show his scrupulous conscientiousness:

FEB. 2.—"Boxes of furniture and books not arrived. Felt great anxiety for the Sabbath. *No sermons. Lord help* me."

That this was a sore trial to him there can be no doubt, for he was deeply impressed with the solemn responsibilities which rest on him who preaches the Word, and never, unless there was a call which he could not decline, ventured into the pulpit without careful and prayerful study. But in this instance, as in all his trials, he looked Above for help and it came. On the following day he wrote:

FEB. 3RD.—"Morning somewhat cloudy and cold. Congregation good— text: I Cor. 11: 1, 5. Had so ne liberty in speaking, but did not feel right to commence my labors here with so little preparation. O God, forgive and bless. At night preached from 'Behold the Lamb of God.'"

For a while he was busily engaged in removing to his new home and fitting it up. This task performed he commenced exploring his field of labor and laid the foundations of his subsequent usefulness by visiting from house to house, forming the acquaintance of his flock, studying their condition and their wants and securing their confidence and affection. His diary, which was kept up, without intermission, from this time till his death, gives us his life in miniature. The entries are brief, recording, for the most part, only the facts and events of his daily life, but they are sufficient to show the man as he was, his zeal and industry, his consecration, his unselfishness, his prayerfulness, his firmness. One day we have a record of visits to the people of his charge, with a brief prayer for God's blessing on each of them. Then in his study laboring lowly and with but partial success to prepare for the Sabbath:

°Felt unusually oppressed in spirit. In my study. An unprofitable day." And again: "In my study all day, but did nothing towards preparation

When Yellow Jack Came Calling...

The *Wilmington Journal* newspaper became so short-handed due to the epidemic that it was reduced to publishing just a single broadside edition bearing news of the newly dead.

1862 BURIAL SITE OF YELLOW FEVER VICTIMS

Communal burial site of approximately 400 people who died of yellow fever during Wilmington's epidemic between September and the frosts of November 1862. Few yellow fever victims' burials are marked with headstones.

In 1862 Wilmington's population, black and white, was approximately 10,000. About half of the population fled the city to avoid the epidemic. Of the 1,505 reported cases, 654 (43%) died of yellow fever.

Oakdale Cemetery in Wilmington is where victims of the epidemic were interred in a mass grave. Today a historical marker remembers the dark days of 1862 that claimed so many lives.

Elizabeth Day's tombstone in Oakdale is one of the very few that dot the large yellow fever burial site. Most who perished did not have anyone left alive who would either remember where they were interred, or who was actually buried in the mass grave.

Dr. James Dickson was one of the few physicians who stayed in the stricken city to do what he could for the scores of dying yellow fever victims. His dedication cost him his life.

Father Thomas Murphy of Wilmin gton's Catholic church was one of the three men of the cloth who stayed to minister to the sick and dying. He is the only one of the three who survived.

Photo courtesy New Hanover County Public Library

St. James Episcopal Church's Rev. R.B. Drane was one of three men of the church, including Rev. John Lamb Prichard, who chose to stay in Wilmington during the epidemic. Like Prichard, Rev. Drane also perished of yellow fever.

Sisters of Mercy nuns from Charleston came to Wilmington to tend to the sick. One of them may have nursed Rev. Prichard when he was struck low.

Photo courtesy New Hanover County Public Library

for the Sabbath. It was one of my dark, unprofitable days. Lord, forgive my unprofitableness."

But these gloomy seasons came only at rare intervals. More frequently he tells of brighter days when he glides smoothly and easily through his task and study is not a weariness to the flesh, as in the following:

"At home in my study, preparing a sermon for the Sabbath, on the 'new birth.' Had a pleasant time."

"A good day—studying text—'He that believeth not shall be damned.' Felt great interest and had more than usual pleasure in preparation."

And again on the next day: "Still engaged in my preparation and did not get through till dinner."

The Sabbath was to him a busy, but delightful day. Always in the Sabbath School, to cheer and encourage by his presence and his example, he often acted as teacher or Superintendent. It was a pleasant place to him. The songs, the faces and voices of the children, and the consciousness that in all which was going on, good seed were being sown in youthful hearts, which were to bring forth fruit unto usefulness here and unto eternal life hereafter, gave to the place and the exercises a charm which often soothed him into forgetfulness of weariness, weakness and care. The Sabbath School over, he entered the pulpit and presented to his congregation the great truths which had occupied his mind during the week. The amount of labor which marked many of his Sabbaths must have taxed his strength to the utmost. It is not strange that he should have been tired and felt little like doing anything on the following day. But we let him speak for himself:

"In Sabbath school as Superintendent, seventy scholars in attendance. Baptized Mrs. M's. servant, an humble looking man. God bless him."

"Visited a Sunday school in the suburbs and opened [illegible text] exercises with prayer. Talked to the children. Visited sister B. who is sinking fast but is strong in faith. Preached to large congregations, in the morning on 'Tyranny of sin;' at night on 'Freedom from sin.' "

The early hours referred to in the next item, were occasioned by the state of the tide, which it was necessary to consult in administering the ordinance.

"Arose at half past four. Repaired to the river and baptized Miss F. A most interesting time. Attended Sunday School. Preached, communion; preached again at 5 o'clock, P. M. Very good congregations."

"Went to Sabbath School. Preached at half past ten o'clock. Held meeting for the colored people in the afternoon. Visited an afflicted lady. Preached at night."

He was always at the weekly prayer-meeting, unless necessarily kept away. It was not a formality, merely a part of his ordinary routine, but a precious season to him. He seemed to realize, and wished to make others realize that the union of brethren in prayer at these stated periods was a living and inestimable privilege. To improve it to the utmost, both for himself and others, was his constant desire.

Once a month came the concert of prayer for Missions which was never forgotten or neglected. The following entry shows how he regarded it:

Monday.- "Felt like resting. At night concert of prayer for Missions. Collected $7.00. Felt that it was good to try to do something for Christ."

From these graver duties, which tasked him heavily, he found recreation in various ways. Reading was a constant source of pleasure to him. He had stocked his library with many of the old authors. These were his familiar companions, his most valued friends, though he kept up with the best periodicals and other literature of the day.

Frequently he was pleasantly diverted from his regular duties by visits from his brethren in the ministry. Few men enjoy such visits more, and his pleasure, manifested in every word and movement, made the visitor feel at home at once. Many, very many, in different parts of the land, will cherish, through life, sunny memories of the genial and hearty hospitality of this servant of God. He was especially gracious to his younger brethren. The struggles and hardships of his early life imparted to his manner towards them much of the tenderness of an elder brother.

Extracts from his diary, such as the following, could be multiplied indefinitely:

"Called to see brethren K— and S—. They walked to my house. The day passed off most pleasantly."

"Went to S. S. Dr. K. addressed the school and preached to a large congregation. Brother S. preached at night."

"Went early to visit the brethren. Made several calls. Church-meeting at night. Received two."

"A rare day! rich in enjoyment. Brethren K—, S— and R—, spent a part of the day with us. So pleasant! Much religious conversation."

Ordinarily these notes are concluded with a prayer that the visit may be blessed to the spiritual good of all the parties.

He was not unfrequently called off to other points to preach occasional sermons or to assist in revivals. Twice this year he went to the assistance of neighboring pastors, once to take part in a revival in Goldsboro. While there he wrote in his diary:

"Left early for Goldsboro. Went to prayer meeting; a very interesting season. Many serious, and some professed."

"Preached last night to a crowded house. Several professed. A very interesting prayer meeting this morning. House nearly filled. I preached; some found peace. Visited some. A glorious time."

"Prayer meeting. O, it was sweet beyond expression. So glad I'm here. The Lord is here. Several professed. Held a meeting for young men, and preached at night."

In May of this year he attended the meeting of the Chowan Association, the first time, we think, that he had visited the body since his connection with it was dissolved. It was a sad and yet a pleasant season with him, and the brief entries in his diary do not express a tithe of what his full heart experienced:

"Arrived at Camden. Met many relatives—mother, brother, sister, &c. Had to preach the introductory sermon—Rom. 3: 25, 26. Took active part in the deliberations on Chowan Female Institute and Reynoldson Institute. Met many old and dear friends. O how delightful thus to meet. Still had much to say for Wake Forest College.

"Sunday. An immense concourse. Brother T. preached first and I followed. Brother T. closed. O God, bless the word. Brother and I went to see cousins G. and M. L. Much pleasant conversation. Cousin C. gave me my note for $25 and interest since Jan. 1839. Lord, reward him. All day at my brother's. Had much conversation about old times and our future prospects. Shall not all meet again on earth!"

"Took leave of my mother and all, and went to Elizabeth City. Preached at night to a crowded house—'Able to save to the uttermost,' &c.

"Reached home, found all well. O God, accept [illegible text] heartfelt thanks, and bless and save us."

In June he attended the Commencement exercises of Wake Forest College, his *Alma Mater,* in whose prosperity he ever felt a deep interest. On his return he wrote:

"Reached home at 6, A. M.—found all well. Feel glad I went. O, that some good may result to me and those whom I met."

In October he attended the session of the Union Association for the first time. In November he was a delegate to the Baptist State Convention of North Carolina, and an active participant in its deliberations. This was one of the most important sessions of that body ever held. Indeed it was the beginning of a new era in the history of the denomination in the State. The addresses which were delivered and the spirit which pervaded the assembly are still remembered by those who were present. The cause of benevolence received an impetus which is felt in some measure even now.

In addition to the usual contributions to missions, $25,000 were secured for the endowment of Wake Forest College, and $13,000 for the erection of a new house of worship in Raleigh. In such an assembly no one [illegible text] more at home than the subject of this memoir; none felt more deeply the importance of the objects under consideration, spoke more earnestly or gave more freely in support of them.

The year closed prosperously for him. His steady perseverance in pursuing his studies under severe trials and great discouragements in early life, the reputation for scholarship and piety, with which he graduated, and his labors in Virginia had prepared the Baptists of North Carolina to receive him favorably. When he came among them once more, his social qualities, chastened and perfected by Divine grace, and the ability and enlightened zeal with which he advocated every good cause, raised still higher their estimate of the man and extended the sphere of his influence and usefulness.

In his pastoral relations he was equally favored. The year was one of arduous labor and of severe trials. He had to explore the ground, seek out and gather together his scattered flock, ascertain their condition and wants, and secure their confidence and affection, so that they would follow and co-operate with him through the coming years. To God he looked for direction in a work so difficult and delicate, and he did not look in vain. Twelve persons were baptized during the year, and its close saw the church revived and united, and the hearts of the people bound to their pastor by ties as strong as death. This last result would have followed in the regular course of things, but it was accomplished much sooner than is usual, and mainly through the blessed ministry of sanctified suffering. Commencing in April and extending through a period of several months are entries in his diary such as the following:

"In my study till 4, P. M., when I attended the funeral of sister B.—text: Psalms 116: 15. Many out. The first of our members buried [illegible text] my settlement here. O that all may be as well prepared as was she. She died in Christ."

"Called early to see Miss C. F." (an estimable young lady, daughter of one of his deacons,) "who is very ill."

"Went to see Miss C.F., found her extremely ill. Conversed and prayed with her. She died at 12, M. I baptized a colored woman at 2, P. M., and preached at night."

"Preached Miss C. F's. funeral sermon— 'Be ye also ready,' &c."

"At four and a half, A. M. Sister J. sent for me to go and pray for her husband. I went, found him very ill, in great axiety. Prayed with him. He died about 12, M. A distressed family! O Lord bless them."

"Made several calls. Found E. T. sick in in bed, but rejoicing in Christ."

"Brother D. very ill. All very much afflicted. Sympathize with them. Little Henry C. died! Called to see the family."

"Preached little H's funeral; then went to Dr. D's. Quite ill. Remained with him most of the day."

"Made many calls. Had religious conversation and prayer with most of the families."

These brief notes express volumes. They tell of the smitten fold and the constant, tender ministrations of the faithful shepherd, pointing the sick and dying to the Friend of sinners, and then turning to the bereaved and sorrowing ones, in their desolation of spirit, with words of tearful sympathy and heavenly consolation. Verily, he had his reward. Soon his time of trial came and he had need of that sympathy which he had so freely extended to others. Nor was it withheld. He notes it thus:

"Quite sick; had a chill and fever last night; sent for Doctor; completely prostrated. Felt I was a worm and no man. Free from pain, but did not sleep any last night. Many sent to inquire, or came to see us."

"Still on my bed, but more comfortable. Many friends called. All seem very kind. Oh! to be humbled and have this affliction sanctified."

"Not quite so well. Quite exhausted. Concluded I could not go out on Sabbath and baptize. Felt disappointed."

How great a trial this was, may be inferred from the fact, that this was the *first* time, as he remarked, that he had ever been prevented from filling his regular Sabbath appointment, from *personal* indisposition. But a greater affliction awaited him. He thus records it: "Little Jemmie," his son, "taken sick."

This little boy nearly five years old, was a specially cherished object of affection because of many little attractive ways, and in view of what seemed to his loving parents to be a peculiar precocity of mind. He had become deeply interested in the exercises of the Sunday school, and was always prepared to repeat his hymn which had been memorized. Though quite sick on Saturday, he was sufficiently improved on Sunday to appear in his class. All the hymns in his book had been previously repeated, up to the 18th, and on this morning, he recited those beautiful lines:

> *"We infants sing,*
> *To Christ our king*
> *A song of praise and love;*
> *The lisping praise*
> *Which now we raise,*
> *Is heard in heaven above.*
> *"Twas babes like us*
> *Whom thou didst bless,*
> *Dear Lord, and honored much.*
> *'Forbid them not'*
> *Were his kind words,*
> *'My kingdom is of such.'*
> *"Kind Savior still*
> *On Zion's hill*
> *Oh, bless our infant band;*
> *And be thou near,*
> *When storms appear*
> *To shield us with thy hand.*

Thus far he repeated. The last verse he was to recite on the following Sunday:

"The ocean crossed,
No wanderer lost,
May we the haven gain,
To join the throng
And swell the song
Of cherubs' raptured strain."

But ere the next meeting of the Sunday school, he had crossed the ocean," had gained the haven, and was swelling the song of the redeemed.

This will prepare the reader to understand the deep feeling with which the father alludes to the brief illness and unexpected death of his darling boy. To return to the diary:

"J. better and went to Sabbath school. 83 scholars. Communion; received seven members Preached twice. J's fever returned; quite sick all night."

"J. no better—worse! Dr. D came 5 or six times. A day of great anxiety. O Lord help us! Save Lord! He is thine. *I will trust in thee, for thou wilt do only right.* O, what a night! Thought J. would die."

"Our dear little Jemmie seemed better—only seemed so, was delighted with flowers a little friend sent him. Soon grew worse and worse until 7, P.M., when he breathed his last! O God be with us for Christ's sake! Friends so kind."

"Our sweet little A. was taken sick at 2, A. M. Lord, we know not what is in the future for us, nor would we. Passing under the rod, and through the deep waters. O Lord, sustain us and sanctify all to our good. Sat up all night."

The following extracts are from letters written during this time of trial. After speaking of the extreme illness of his little son, he writes:

"Everything was done, no doubt, that could be. Many of our brethren and sisters came in and manifested all possible kindness. He continued to grow worse until about one, A. M., when it seemed he must sink, unless some relief could be given. It was a most solemn time. All the children were called up, as we supposed, to see our sweet little Jemmie die. But presently the blisters drew and that seemed to revive him. He had

failed to recognize us, and could not talk. While Sister C. was dressing his blisters his consciousness and speech returned. This morning he seemed more quiet and indeed much better; but he is far from being out of danger, now past 3, P. M. Much and fervent prayer has been, and still is offered for his recovery."

The hopes of all were disappointed, and in a few hours the little sufferer passed from his earthly home to one in heaven, to be followed in a few short years by his devoted father. Together, their earthly forms rest in Oakdale Cemetery, Wilmington, far from kindred, but among those, some of whom, at least, will long remember the faithful ministry of their devoted pastor. To a friend he wrote:

AUG. 9th— "A. is certainly better. We feel much encouraged to hope that she will soon be up again. Our friends are *so kind.* They do all they can to assuage our grief. I am sure they truly sympathize with us. We are trying to bear our affliction with becoming resignation. I desire to learn the lesson God would teach us. * * * Our sweet little Jemmie is buried in brother F's. lot in the cemetery. His coffin is enclosed in a strong box, with reference to having it removed to my own ground after awhile."

We resume the extracts from the journal:

AUG. 9th.—At home all day. Felt lonely. Afflicted."

10th.—Made some remarks at Sunday School. Much affected, so were all. Preached—Rom. viii: 17. Felt somewhat relieved. Brother R. preached at 5 P. M. Many friends called in after preaching."

"Rode to the cemetery with wife, sister and little A. We went to our little J's. grave.

'Thou art gone to the grave,
But we will not deplore thee.'

Attended the funeral of Brother B. at 9, A. M. After coming home had a chill. Felt discouraged."

He and each member of his family were quite sick for several days. In this season of suffering and anxiety he wrote:

"Thus all are being afflicted to-night. Lord help us, we've no other help."

The storm could not last forever. He, who holds the seas in the hollow of his hands, spoke and the winds were hushed into silence, and the glad sunshine and the fair sky appeared again, wearing a milder, softer loveliness than ever before. The dawning of this brighter day is thus recorded:

"Felt quite feeble. Went into Sunday School. Much affected, hearing the singing. Thought of dear little J. Preached from 'If any man will come after me, &c.' Communion. Only one service."

"Felt thankful that the health of my family and my own is much better. Reading in my study, and feel that I enjoy it, after a long interruption. Arranged my thoughts for the Sabbath. O, to be prepared."

With the return of health to himself and his family he devoted himself with subdued and chastened spirit but with renewed energy to his legitimate work. His afflictions had been severe but he neither murmured nor complained. He recognized the hand of God in them all and believed what he now sees from the serene and blissful home which filled so large a place in his heart while on earth, that they were sent in infinite wisdom and infinite love. The prayer, which he so frequently offered up, that these trials might be sanctified to his own good and that of the church, was heard and granted. His ministrations at the bedside of the sick and the dying, and his words of comfort to the bereaved ones gave him a firm hold on every heart, on some who could not have been reached in any other way. In like manner their kindness to him when he was passing through the deep waters endeared them to him by ties which neither toil, nor care nor the flight of years could sever or loosen. He purchased a lot in Oakdale Cemetery and transferred little Jemmie's remains to it. Thenceforward Wilmington seemed to be the home of his heart as it had been in reality before. He felt that here his earthly labors for the Master were to end. How true! Alas, that they should have ended so soon! The following entries are found at this time in his diary:

"I have removed the remains of my dear child to the new lot! I feel so thankful it is done. 'There sweet be his rest, &c.' I went to the cemetery twice to-day.

17th.—With brother Mitchell, agent for W. F. College. I do not enjoy this so well, but it must be done, the college must be endowed.

22nd.—I went to the cemetery and saw the tombstone erected by the Sunday School of Front Street Baptist Church, to the memory of our dear little James.

23rd.—Intensely cold, blowing almost a gale. In doors all day. Much interested in reading the Christian Review. Sat up late and read aloud in 'Rise of the Dutch Republic.'

27th.—Made up a little amount to present to a brother minister. Found no difficulty at all. O, there is a real pleasure in trying to do good!

28th.—Beautiful morning—in the Sunday School.—Preached on *Retrospection.* 'Thou shalt remember all the way, &c.'

29th.—Church meeting—large number out—did much business.

30th.—Met the committee to consult about building a new church."

The new year dawned on a happy christian household. The old year had seen them sorely tried under the chastening rod, and from that little group one cherished form had gone out to return never more. But faith had recognized in these trials the Hand that doth not willingly afflict, and this morning, as they gathered around the family altar, gratitude for past mercies and blessings, and hope for the future filled each heart. What a pleasing picture is presented in the following brief extract from Mr. P's. diary,

"1857 Jan. 1st.—Arose early and all the family joined in reading the first chapter of Genesis. Sung a new year's hymn and prayed."

All through this year he was earnestly engaged in efforts to promote the spiritual well being of the church. These efforts, if judged by the apparent and immediate results, were only partially successful. But his labor was not in vain in the Lord. The blessing was delayed for a while but came in rich measure at length.

We introduce a few items from the diary of this year, illustrating something of the nature of his varied employments. Attendance at the commencement of Wake Forest College is thus referred to:

"**JUNE 10th,**—To day Dr. Hooper delivered a very able address, on 'The sacredness of human life and American disregard of it.' Had interesting conversation with brethren.

11th.—Commencement day. Six graduates."

On reaching home he wrote:

"**13th.**—Remained at home all day, trying to get ready for Sabbath. Felt very tired.

23d.—Making arrangements for Sabbath School picnic.

24th.—Pleasant morning. Feel so thankful. Sabbath School met at the church and went to the 'Oaks.' Mr. F. made a speech at 11 o'clock and we had dinner about 12 1-2. At least 150 present. All passed off very pleasantly. Got home about 5 P. M.

JULY 1st.—In my study, preparing sermon on the subject of *Election*— that much misunderstood doctrine.

5th.—Ninety-one scholars at Sunday School. Preached on *Election*. A very large and attentive congregation. Attended funeral at 4 1-2 o'clock, P. M. Baptized, at 5 1-2, six colored persons. Preached at night on *Election*— crowd.

6th.—Felt so much better than I expected. Worked in my flower garden till 9. Went to Post Office. Spent the day in reading and writing.

7th—Endeavoring to prepare to meet the most plausible objections to the doctrine of *election*.

8th.—Delightful morning, so cool and pleasant. Little J. quite unwell—went for the doctor. Busily engaged in Sabbath preparations, particularly in an endeavor to show, that though there are mysteries and difficulties connected with Election, yet not more than with other doctrines received. It is to be believed, not understood.

10th. 'O Lord, how manifold are thy mercies' Little J. is better. The other children well. Spent the day in reading.

12th.—Preached—'Objections to Election considered,' preliminary to a fuller answer to-night. Preached to-night.

15th.—In my study all day, reading and arranging for a sermon, on the *importance of a right understanding of doctrines, in order to peace of mind and happiness.*

26th.—Baptized three colored persons.

31st.—Took M. and R. and went to Lenoir county, *via* Goldsboro. At Mosely Hall, met many of the brethren and sisters, Went to brother W's—how pleasant a family. What fields of cotton and corn, and plenty of fruit.

AUGUST 2nd.—Sabbath. Brother G. preached from I. Kings viii: 26. I preached from 'Mercy and truth are met, &c.'

5th—Dear little James died one year ago to-day. Returned home.

8th.—Spent the morning in study. The health of all is quite good now. I desire to be truly thankful for all our mercies.

12th—Feel quite feeble. Called to see Mr. H.; delivered W's. dying message to him. Talked and prayed with him. It is very warm. Shall endeavor to keep close in the house out of the sun. O Lord, grant me and my family health and strength to labor for thee.

23rd.—Sabbath. One hundred and four in Sunday School; good congregation. Preached from Psalm viii: 8. Enjoyed the services very much. A good day. Lord, bless."

Some months after his death, a gentleman hearing his name mentioned, remarked: "Being detained in Wilmington once, I attended the Baptist church and heard Mr. P. preach on the proper observance of the Sabbath. I was at that time connected with the railroad, and compelled to travel on the Sabbath. I was convinced by his sermon that I could not consistently continue in this business, and so resigned my situation."

"30th.—Preached on 'Observance of Lord's Day,' and at night on 'Taking the name of God in vain.' I enjoyed the day very much. O that a rich blessing may attend the labors of God's people."

Early in the Spring of the following year, 1858, Wilmington was visited with the most remarkable religious awakening ever known in that city. It extended to all the religious denominations, and continued more than two months. For a time religion was the most prominent topic of thought and conversation among all classes of the citizens. The Baptist churches shared largely in these gracious influences. The First church was especially favored. Her strength was much increased, whether we consider the numbers added to her fold or the renewed spiritual life imparted to the whole body.

Mr. P's. diary, as illustrating his mode of life at this time:

"11th.—In my study and found it good to make preparation for to-night. Felt a deep interest in being prepared for this meeting. I was also studying Ps. cxxxiii, for Sabbath morning. O God, give me and give us all, as a church, the goodness and pleasantness and the blessing of that Psalm. There was quite a good number out at night and I enjoyed the meeting very much.

12th.—A most delightful day in my study. Sat up till eleven reading 'Livingstone's travels in South Africa.' It is a thrilling book. O, that there were more Bowens, Livingstones, &c. Lord, send many good men to Africa.

13th.—I spent the entire day with my family, in reading the papers, Recorder, Herald, Journal of Commerce, &c., &c. It was a rare treat for me and I enjoyed it much. It was stormy *without,* but a good coal fire, healthy, playful children and affectionate wife, made it sunshiny *within.* A sweet day. Lord, sanctify it to us all.

14th.—Sabbath. Text—cxxxiii Psalm. O, it was a sweet time to me, and I think to many. May it indeed prove a great blessing to the church. Preached at night on 'Transfiguration.' Congregation very attentive.

18th.—In my study. Could not get my mind interested as I sometimes have it. There was a dullness, a sluggishness, which I could not overcome. O, to be free from these clogs.

19th.—How different a day from yesterday. I can truly say, I felt it good to be here. Had to read much in relation to my subject.

21st.—Went early, at eight, to attend a funeral. Back to Sunday School; one hundred and forty-three present.—Preached—Luke xvii: 2. At 2, P.M., attended a funeral over the Railroad. Preached at night.

26th. Borrowed a volume of Webster's works, and read his argument on the Girard College, to my great delight and, I trust, profit. Read several articles bearing on the christian ministry, and then commenced preparing a discourse on that subject, and continued until eleven and could have continued much longer, but felt I ought to sleep.

28th.—A lovely morning. One hundred and thirty-three in Sunday School. A large congregation. Preached on the 'Christian Ministry, its nature, object and claims,' Isa. lii: 9, Nahum I: 15, Rom. x: 15. Took up a collection for our Beneficiaries, $28. At 2, P. M., baptized two persons. A very large crowd and very good attention. Attended my Bible class, rested a little and preached again at night.

MARCH 5th.—In my study, finished my sermon for Sunday morning, and after dinner commenced one for the night. Spent the evening reading the papers. Amidst all my cares and anxieties, I have my joys and delights.

14th.—One of the loveliest of mornings. So clear, mild and calm. The beautiful river reflects every object. One hundred and twenty in Sunday School. A large congregation and very attentive. 'Behold I lay in Zion, for a foundation, a stone, &c.' Bible class at three. A goodly number out. Enjoyed it much. Lord bless these humble efforts. Preached at night from, 'If any man build upon this foundation, &c.' Read till eleven."

The beginnings of the gracious revival to which we have referred above are indicated in the extracts which follow:

"**15th.**—Rose at five and felt entirely refreshed by sleep. The most spring-like morning yet. Went to prayer-meeting. About twenty-three out and a most delightful time. Called to see Mr. M., talked and prayed; and at brother A's., talked and prayed. Went to Dr. D's. prayer-meeting, prayed. Thirty-three ladies at Society. Went to brother R's. meeting."

"**MARCH 16th.**—At sunrise prayer-meeting again this morning. About forty-five persons there. It was a precious season. At night preached from Rev. ii: 5. The congregation was large and attentive. Three knelt for prayer. Lord, bless all."

"**MARCH 17th.**—At sunrise prayer-meeting again. A large number out. It was one of the sweetest meetings I ever attended. Preached at night from Isaiah 53: 12. Several knelt for prayer."

"**MARCH 23rd.**—Cloudy and raining hard, but a large congregation at the prayer-meeting. It was a melting time. O for the Spirit's power. Lord, grant it to thy people to-day. Preached at night—text, Matt. 11: 27, 30. A precious meeting. Lord bless the efforts."

"**APRIL 15th.**—Just one month ago we commenced our sunrise prayer-meetings. This morning we came together to thank God for what he had already done for us all. A more delightful season I have not yet enjoyed."

Thus the record runs on through April and May. The sunrise prayer meeting was the first labor of the day. Then visiting among his people till 10, A. M., or 12, M., when he usually attended a prayer-meeting in another part of the city. In the afternoon a brief interval of rest, then among his people again, and in the pulpit at night. The labor was herculean, but he loved it, and it was not till near the close that he showed signs of failing strength. His diary makes occasional mention of assistance from visiting ministers, as in the following:

"**MARCH 30th.**—Brother McA—, of Sampson, took tea with us, and preached at night. 'Be ye also ready.' A heavenly meeting."

"**APRIL 27th.**—Brother K—y, of Duplin, preached—Eph. 3: 8. A good sermon. Congregation large, serious and attentive. Many asked for prayer in their behalf."

These visits of his brethren in the ministry were very refreshing to him, but they did not come often during the progress of this gracious work. Most of the time he was alone.

Two letters of his written at this period have been preserved. We make the following extracts:

WILMINGTON, MAY 21ST, 1858.

"* * * * * *I was truly glad to hear of the interest in the college and in the Grace Street Church. O, that it may become more deep and general. I am sorry I have not time now to answer J's. letter. I remember preaching from the text to which he alludes. I believed it then, I know it now. We still continue our morning prayer-meetings, and they are still very interesting and profitable to many of us. Several say, 'Don't give them up.' On Wednesday night we held a meeting for attending to the regular business of the church. My heart was deeply affected when I saw so many there, members of the church, who a short time ago were in their sins. Our meeting was a delighful one. The interest has very sensibly subsided, but there is a very happy state of things and several are anxious. * * *
I feel amazed at myself, that I have not felt more the effects of my arduous and protracted labors. I have determined to take a week or two of rest, lest I should not be able to stand the warmer weather that is now at hand. I now think of leaving home on Monday week for Richmond; thence to the General Association of Virginia; and from thence to Commencement at Wake Forest. Do not feel disappointed if I do not come, for life and health are very uncertain. I anticipate no little pleasure, however, if it be*

the will of God to permit me to visit you all once more and to see the brethren whom I so much love in the Lord."

* * * * * * * *

The text alluded to in the above letter was: "They that sow in tears shall reap in joy." He *knew* by experience the truth of the declaration in the happy revival through which he had just passed.

WILMINGTON, MAY 14TH, 1858.

"*MY DEAR —: Your very welcome letter was received, and we were truly glad to hear of the welfare of the family, and also the encouraging prospects of the Foreign Mission Board. I trust I do feel a deep interest in all that relates to the Redeemer's kingdom at home and abroad. Since I last wrote, nothing of special interest has occurred in our meetings. Sunday was indeed a delightful day with us as a church. It is so different from what it used to be. The young men's prayer-meeting is very interesting, many of the young men praying and giving a word of exhortation. There is a very interesting state of things among our colored people in all the churches. There were thirty or forty anxious enquirers in our church, Sunday afternoon. I could not attend. Several of the brethren met with them and the colored brethren mostly conducted their own meetings. Our sunrise prayer-meetings are still continued, though by no means so largely attended as formerly. But I think they are sweeter, if possible, than before.*

Last night we had a thanksgiving meeting to return God special thanks for what he had done for our town and especially for our church. And notwithstanding Dr. Hawks lectured before the 'Mount Vernon Association,' we had a very large congregation and the services were of a most interesting character. The singing was spirited, the prayers fervent, and the remarks of some of the young converts most impressive. An old man, a sailor for over thirty years, and a Catholic—a Scotchman by birth, spoke of his thankfulness to God that he had been permitted to live to attend this meeting and find the Saviour, &c. * * * *

Most sincerely do we sympathize with sister R. and all the family in the loss of one so dear to us all. But no! she is not lost, even to us. 'She is not dead but sleepeth.' Present to the afflicted family our kindest regards.

We thought and spoke of you all yesterday and last night. May God bless our dear brother and sister and make them a great blessing to one another and to many others. Love to all.

Truly yours,

J. L. PRICHARD."

On the 31st of May he writes in his diary:

"Awoke early. Thought of the sunrise prayer-meetings which I had been attending so long and with so much pleasure and profit. Lifted my heart to God in supplication for all who attended them."

The daily meetings are over. During their continuance nearly one hundred members have been added to the church, and the whole body has been awakened into new life and activity. The pastor, worn down by excessive labor, needed recreation; and on the 2nd of June he took leave of his family and flock to attend the meeting of the General Association of Virginia at Hampton. After a brief sojourn among his friends in the Old Dominion he returned to his home by way of Wake Forest college, where he stopped to attend the Commencement exercises and preach the sermon before the graduating class. In July he attended the Commencement exercises of the Chowan Female Collegiate Institute, Murfreesboro, N. C. While there he wrote to his daughter the letter which we give below:

(TO HIS DAUGHTER.)

MURFREESBORO, JULY 7TH, 1859.

*"MY DEAR M.:—You can scarcely conceive how much you were contributing to the happiness of your father when on Monday last, you penned those lines at home. I am very much obliged to you, dear child, for your affectionate letter. I am glad you have vacation, so that you can rest awhile. * * * * Thinking it may interest you, I will say a few words in reference to the Institute at this place. It is a large and beautiful building, situated from a half to three fourths of a mile from the village. The grounds are beautifully laid out, and beautiful elm trees are planted in such a*

manner as to represent the planets. This was Mr. Fory's taste. There are about ten acres connected with the Institute, so that the young ladies can walk miles, within their own grounds. Besides, the college building has porticoes, extending the entire length, which afford a good place for exercise in damp or rainy weather. The chapel is a beautiful room, containing a large organ.

*I was present at the Commencement. The music was good so far as the instrumental part was concerned. There are eighty pupils connected with the school. There were thirteen graduates. It was an interesting sight, to see thirteen young ladies, dressed in white, standing up to receive their diplomas. The essays were good. Dr. Hooper's address to the graduating class was excellent. Dr. Kean's address was also very good. His subject was 'Development, Physical, Mental and Moral.' I have no doubt this is a fine institution. I should be glad to have you come here or to some other such school and complete your studies. I shall try to give you as good an education as my means will allow. I doubt not, my dear child, you will endeavor to improve your golden opportunities. One thing Dr. Hooper said last night, I regretted to hear, that so 'many of the young ladies had not made choice of the better part which Mary chose.' My daughter, 'with all thy gettings, get wisdom.' I feel great anxiety about this. Do try, my dear, and give your whole heart to the Saviour. Love him now. * * * * * ***

I am, dear Mary, your affectionate father."

CHAPTER VII.

NEW HOUSE OF WORSHIP IN WILMINGTON—ENTERPRISE
DIFFICULT—INCREASED LABORS AND SOLICITUDE OF
PASTOR—EXTRACTS FROM DIARY—CONDITION OF THE
COUNTRY—LOVE OF THE UNION—EXTRACTS FROM DIARY—
WAR—WORK AMONG THE SOLDIERS—AFFECTING INCIDENT—
EXTRACTS FROM DIARY—LETTERS—VISIT TO RICHMOND—
TESTIMONY OF A SOLDIER.

When Mr. P. took charge of the church in Wilmington it was with the understanding that they would build a larger and better house of worship, on a more eligible site, as the one in which they were then worshipping was not at all adequate to the wants of the denomination in that growing city. His attention was never diverted from this object, though, from various causes, no formal action in the matter was taken by the church for more than a year after the settlement of the new pastor among them. Towards the close of 1857 they began to consider the matter in earnest, and early in 1858 a lot on the corner of Fifth and Market streets was purchased. In the Fall of this year Mr. P., with one of the deacons of the church, visited Richmond, Baltimore, Washington and other cities, examining models and consulting architects, with the view of securing the best plan for their new edifice. In February 1859 the subscription list was opened, and pledges to the amount of $10,000 were secured the first day. He then engaged diligently in the work of collection and canvassed the city with considerable success. All that could be raised at home was secured and the building was commenced. Subsequently he visited many portions of the State, soliciting contributions in behalf of the enterprise, and though he often encountered indifference or opposition yet each trip swelled the amount of funds. Slowly but surely the work went forward till the breaking out of the war and the blockade of our ports rendered it impossible to procure the necessary materials.

This new undertaking illustrates the character of the man. It was of sufficient magnitude to discourage one who had less earnestness and faith. The requisite amount of funds could not be raised in Wilmington, and the slow and tedious process of soliciting aid from abroad must be resorted to. This part of the labor he must perform. He encountered indifference or opposition at home. Much more must he expect it in communities that had no local interest in the enterprise. His pastoral labors were heavy, and to these must be added the task of surpervising the work as it progressed, and of travelling over the State to collect money. The danger of failure on the one hand and the magnitude of the work on the other, might well have made him shrink back and wait for a more convenient season. But he neither gave up the scheme nor even hesitated about it. The house was needed. It was to be built for God and God would provide the means. So he reasoned and so he acted, and subsequent events have shown that he was right. The work which was suspended by the war has been vigorously prosecuted by his successor, Rev. W. M. Young, and there is every prospect of its completion at an early day. We give a few extracts from Mr. P's. diary to show the views and feelings with which he began and prosecuted the enterprise:

"Spent the whole evening in conversation with the brethren in reference to building a church, buying a lot, &c., &c. O God, help us to build a good house and pay for it and worship thee in it. Wilt thou not?"

"Early the sisters commenced coming to form a society, according to appointment, to raise funds for the church. Nineteen names given in. A pleasant meeting."

Again, before meeting the brethren for consultation, he wrote:

"Lord, grant us thy wisdom for Jesus' sake."

Again he wrote:

"I am about to start once more to solicit aid to build a house for the Lord. O Lord, the gold and the silver and the hearts of men are thine. Thou canst dispose them aright. Help me for Jesus' sake to succeed this day."

"Hope to be able to do something to-day for the Lord's house. O God, prepare me to labor, and the hearts of the people to give liberally."

Later in the day he states the amount received, and adds:

"I feel very thankful for these sums and encouraged—confident that my prayer was answered."

"Wrote a piece for each of the daily papers in behalf of the new church enterprise. Saw several of the members in relation to subscriptions and secured $700 before 2, P. M."

With these aims and in this spirit he labored on, and the measure of success which crowned his efforts was all that could have been expected. How could it have been otherwise?

To raise the money as it was needed, and give his personal attention to the work on the new building as it progressed made large demands on his time, but he did not on this account neglect his pastoral duties. He was as careful as ever in the preparation of his sermons and as punctual in visiting the people of his charge. Nor did he or his church, though so heavily taxed, forget the great objects of christian beneficence. Their contributions in behalf of missions, both at home and abroad, were as frequent and liberal as ever.

We turn now to his diary for 1860. The entries are more copious and give us a clearer view of his life and character during the eventful months that followed:

"**Jan. 7th.**—Enjoyed family prayers. I know not how any Christian family can dispense with family worship and live as a Christian desires to live inwardly! How does he keep the fire always burning on the altar of his heart? I feel I need it.

14th.—I am very much pleased with my new Atlas by Mitchell. I feel more than ever the importance of a knowledge of Geography. I intend to give more attention to it than I have done and encourage my children to do so.

31st.—Reading the Eclectic Magazine and was truly edified and instructed. O, that I had more time to read.

Feb. 8th.—I do not think it easy to over estimate the importance of a knowledge of Geography and History and deeply regret my limited knowledge of both. I will try even now, at *the age of forty-nine,* to correct this deficiency. I rejoice that my children are enjoying advantages which I did not. But I would only know these things to be more useful.

10th.—I know not when I had so pleasant a time with my books, as I have had to day. O Lord, I thank thee for these bunches of grapes from Eshcol.

19th.—At Sabbath school. Had some good singing and enjoyed it much. Preached from Song of Solomon, I: 6. 'But my vineyard I have not kept!' The congregation attentive. I felt more than usual. Rested awhile and read from A. Fuller's and John Howe's works in reference to 'future punishment,' and preached at night from Isaiah X: 14. Congregations good and very attentive.

20th.—Church meeting tonight. A good number out and a very pleasant time. O, I do pray that we may be kept in the bonds of peace. Lord, help us to keep the unity of the Spirit, &c. I feel the deepest anxiety for the church."

After a day of visiting, he writes: "I enjoyed my visits very much. O that good may result. I am more and more convinced of the great good that may be accomplished by *pastoral visiting.* Help me, O Lord, to do my duty."

"22nd.—Enjoyed the work of the day very much. There is nothing like having the heart in our work, giving ourselves wholly to these things. I do trust that my brethren and sisters may be half as much edified in *hearing,* as I was in preparing.

MARCH 8th.—A goodly number out at prayer-meeting. Commented on 'Why should a living man complain?' Enjoyed the exercises and trust others did. May we all cease to complain and be cheerful and be resigned.

16th.—Our dear little J. was so much better that I brought him down stairs to-day. He was delighted. I think that A. and G. are taking measles. O Lord, be pleased to spare them, for us. Make them thine for Jesus sake.

19th.—Bought fruit cake, &c. for Johnnie's birthday. He is four years old. Lord, bless the dear child and help us train him for Thee.

24th.—My throat is worse. Could not sing this morning! It seems strange to have morning prayers without singing. I regard it as a most interesting part of family worship. In my study continued to read and arrange for Sabbath. Find it much easier to prepare a sermon by writing, than in another way. I can think more readily, and become more interested. It is hard to break off from old habits, good or bad. Hence the importance of forming right habits at first.

APRIL 5th.—A day of barrenness. I could not get my mind interested in anything. I wonder if any good minister of the gospel experiences anything like this. O, that I may be delivered from this deadness. 'My soul cleaveth unto the dust, quicken thou me according to thy word.' Saviour, precious Saviour, come to my rescue.

MAY 4th.—Walked to the church. The workmen are laying brick. The walls are rising. Yet I hope to see them rise.

6th.—Sweet little Georgie's birthday; two years old. A calm and lovely Sabbath morning. The birds sing very sweetly. The children are well and happy. Now O Lord, come and fill our hearts with heavenly mindedness and peace and joy, even the joy of the Holy Ghost. Went to Sabbath school; not quite a hundred out. We sang two or three pieces. A large congregation. Preached from Col. II: 9, 10. Communion, a very pleasant time. Received Sister W. who was baptized 24th April.

7th.—Made this a rest day in part. Spent the time in reading. It seems very strange to me to be resting. Enternity for rest."

This month he attended the Chowan Association in Edenton, obtaining more funds for the church.

JUNE 21st.—Saw brother H. Had conversation with him about doing good—mentioned to him how—by buying me some books, now selling at cost at Pierce's. He agreed and I selected the books, $20 worth, 16 volumes. Brought them home and opened them. Children with me much delighted.

JULY 19th.—Called in to see a poor man without Christ and no heart to desire Him! Talked to him kindly. Then went to see brother Harry, (a colored brother.) What a contrast. He is prepared, come what will. He is a calm and peaceful and happy man. Went to church. Saw the door sills, which had just arrived in the steamer 'Parkersburg.' 'I delight in the stones thereof,' Ps. civ: 14, (of the house of God.)

21st.—They have raised the window frames on the west side of the church. I was so glad to see it.

JULY 29th.—At night preached from Jer. viii: 20. This service was peculiarly affecting to me as I expected to be absent for several weeks. O, I felt deeply. Shall we all meet again? O, what shall betide us? Hush, my soul!

AUG. 3rd.—Left home on a trip to secure funds for building our church edifice.

On the 2d of September, after returning from one of his trips to collect funds, he writes: "Attended the funeral of old Sister V. Preached at 10 —'The love of Christ constraineth us.' Communion. An interesting time. Preached again at night. This has been a day full of enjoyment to me. One month since I preached on Sunday to my congregation! I feel this absence from home was a great sacrifice, but a necessary one. I have made it cheerfully."

5th.—Spent the day at home resting. A rarity for me. Well, I do not think I feel as well as if I had been at work all the time.

9th.—Spent the early morning in my study, then to Sabbath school. Enjoyed preaching. At 4, P. M., baptized M. B. A solemn time. Preached again at night.

14th.—A very pleasant day in my study. Found it good to be engaged in my work. At such a time, 'I had rather be a doorkeeper in the house of my God, than to enjoy all that the world can do for me. It is sweet to have a few moment,' foretaste of heaven? 'O heaven, sweet heaven, when shall I see, O when shall I be there!'

15th.—Late in the afternoon I walked again to the church. They have just commenced the vestibule wall. The outer walls are now up to the height of gallery, and soon the gallery will be raised. O Lord, help us to build and pay for this house and give it and ourselves to thee forever.

17th.—I know not when I ever enjoyed reading anything more than the Life of Richard Knill. O to be like him, because he was so much like Christ. Walked to the church. Commenced reading Doddridge's life. Talked with the young ladies about being useful and happy.

22nd.—At 2, P. M., took all the dear children to see the Panorama of Pilgrim's Progress. They have just returned delighted.

28th.—I am so glad brother — has determined to go to the Theological Seminary. O that I could have enjoyed such an advantage in the early part of my ministry. But as I could not, I desire to encourage all young men who can, to go. The Lord bless our young brother.

29th.—This has been a day of unusual anxiety. I just begin to realize that M'. (his daughter) "is going off to School! O Lord, I pray thee, bless my child. Make her a christian. I do give her to thee, thine she is. O make her a dear child of Jesus. I desire to consecrate myself and family anew to Thee. Bless us and make us a blessing!"

During the session of the N. C. Baptist State Convention in Goldsboro he made the following entry:

"**Nov. 3rd.**—At the assembling of the Convention I was allowed to explain in reference to our enterprise of building a church. Received about $265 in cash and subscriptions. Many pleasing events occurred, especially the effort by which the debt of the church in Goldsboro was nearly liquidated. I have never attended a more harmonious session than this has been. Grant, Lord, that it may be the beginning of better times."

About this time the clouds, which afterwards gathered into such a terrific storm and swept in desolating fury over the South, began to appear above the political horizon. No man more clearly understood their dreadful portent or strove more earnestly to avert the impending evil than the subject of this memoir. He was ardently attached to the Union and, while he could, sought to preserve the government under which our country had risen to such greatness and glory. But when the issue came and he must take the part either of the North or the South in the struggle, he could not hesitate. When Virginia and North Carolina cast their fortunes with the Confederate States, he approved their action, and thenceforward the Southern cause had no more devoted adherent and supporter than he. Committing the cause of his country, as he did everything else, to God, he did not despond even in the darkest hour of the fearful and bloody struggle. With this brief explanation we continue our extracts from his diary:

"**Nov. 7th.**—The telegraph says that Lincoln is elected President! The deepest feeling is manifested by all. *Secession* is talked of. O God, undertake for us, we beseech Thee.

8th.—At prayer meeting. But few out. 'Blessed are the peacemakers.' Spoke of the political excitement—urged upon all to be careful to use no exciting language—'*grievous words.*' I am not afraid. Jehovah reigns! Our trust be in Him alone.

15th.—Went to the new church—it has grown some. But O, I feel so sad at the thought of the troublous times. Lord shall the work cease? O let it not, I pray Thee! * * * I *feel profoundly the importance* of this crisis in political matters. O God, forsake us not. Give us men for the times.

16th —The morning is bright and lovely, but the political sky is dark and lowering! Men's hearts tremble for fear; deep mutterings are heard from the South. It does seem that a dissolution of the glorious Union is inevitable! * * * *

18th.—Preached from Jeremiah xviii: 7, 11, in reference to our national affairs. I urged moderation and deliberation, and above all to *distrust man,* all mere parties &c., and to trust in God, to pray to him, have faith in him.

20th. * * * Feel sad—no desire to be in company. I feel it is a time for prayer, meditation and deep humiliation before God. Lord, humble our hearts before thee as a nation. I pray that thou wilt avert the threatened danger.

26th.—Was called upon to attend the funeral of Mr. B.—a sad time, but few there. I walked to the the cemetery. I went to the grave of our darling little James! Sweet child, how calm is thy rest. Revolutions may come, but not to thee. No, thou art beyond them all, safe in the bosom of Jesus. Rest, my child! We will all try and meet thee ere long! Lord, save us all as a family! Let none be lost. Save us from our sins through Jesus' blood.

DEC. 21st.—Walked round by the church. At work on west side, turning arches over the windows. * * * Heard cannon firing at the news of the secession of South Carolina.

The next entry in his diary refers to "six or seven nationalities." This is explained by the fact, not only that Wilmington is a sea port city, but that the Baptist house of worship was near the river and occupied an elevated position. It was no uncommon thing to have quite a number of seamen as his hearers, and he always felt a special interest in their welfare.

23d.—Preached to at least six or seven nationalities, Norwegians, Scotch, Swedes, Prussians, &c. Text, Ps. lxxxv: 6. 'Wilt thou not revive us again?' Without notes—enjoyed it very much and believe most of the hearers did also. I never felt more in praying for *'our country,' 'my country.'* Congregation very large in the morning, and at night good. The singing was truly delightful.

DEC. 25th.—A dark, dreary day. Remained at home, reading the news. There is a war spirit all over the world. China has a double war, Africa is at war, all Europe is stirred to its deepest foundations, and our own America is in a most perilous condition. Nothing but Divine interposition can save us from *war*—internecine war!

29th. * * * South Carolina has declared herself independent. Will the General Government allow it? If not, what then? War? I suppose so. Lord, undertake for us.

30th.—Preached at night from 'Harvest is past, &c.' It was truly a solemn time. I think all felt deeply on taking leave of the last Sabbath in the year. It is a solemn thought—how have I lived?

31st. * * * * All is confusion and uncertainty. South Carolina is precipitating things, and thus goes down the sun on Dec. 31st, 1860. How will it rise and set to-morrow*?* Will it behold our country stained with blood? God forbid it, we pray.

FEB 1st, 1861.—I enter to-day on my sixth year as pastor in this place. How many more shall I be here? Lord help me to be faithful, more than ever. Went to see brother Harry, (an aged colored member) he sleeps sweetly in death.

April 13th.—*Fort Sumter bombarded all night!* Every body is excited. War has commenced; when will it end? Sumter surrendered unconditionally, by Major Anderson, commander! Great rejoicing in Wilmington, flag raising, &c. The windows on towers of our church raised to-day. So glad.

15th.—Lincoln's proclamation received, saying he would order out 75,000 men to take the forts, &c. Greatest excitement on the streets.

21st.—A most lovely morning, but O my soul, what a spectacle does our country present! God have mercy on us! I preached and talked to a good congregation—a deeply solemn time. Text:—Deut. xxxiii: 26, 29. At night, from Job ii: 10.

22d.—Companies from West and South concentrating * * * * Went on the roof of our new church."

During the year 1861 the work on the house progressed slowly and his pastoral duties were attended to as usual. In addition to this, a wider field of usefulness was opened to him among the troops that were concentrated about Wiimington from the commencement of the war, and he was not slow to enter and occupy it.

Every one remembers the eagerness with which the Southern soldiers, suddenly gathered into the camp from the pursuits and pleasures of home, sought for reading-matter with which to relieve the tedium of their daily life. It was Mr. P's. custom to visit them daily, taking with him such magazines, pamphlets, &c., as he could spare from his own library or could collect from others. Thus, by becoming acquainted with the men and manifesting his interest in them, he induced them to attend preaching at the Baptist church; and his congregation which had been thinned by the war, removal of families, and other causes, was greatly increased. His regular services at such times often had a special adaptation to the condition and wants of the soldiers. He frequently conducted religious exercises in the various camps around the city, and as regiments were passing through on their way to the scene of strife he met them at the depot and distributed tracts and Testaments among them, and by pleasant words and many little kind offices assured them of his regard for their spiritual welfare. He was also careful of the physical comfort of the soldiers. They always received a cordial welcome to his house and his table. On many occasions he took sick soldiers to his home that they might enjoy the kind attentions of his family. One of these recipients of his generosity, a young man from Virginia, had no sooner left the hospital than he exclaimed—feeling doubtless that he was with one who could sympathize with him and instruct him in the right way—"Now I think I can give my heart to the Saviour." He had received a letter from his mother, a short time before, informing him of the death of his only brother and urging him to seek the salvation of his soul; and he seemed deeply convicted indeed. Though suffering much bodily pain he seemed to think only of his soul's danger. Mr. P. wrote to the young man's mother: "Though I have been a pastor twenty years, I have never seen any one more penitent and humble."

It soon became evident that he could not recover, and during his last hours he was constantly ministered to by Mr. P. and his family in the tenderest and most faithful manner. His dying whisper—realized we trust—was: "O Heavenly Father, save me." The letter to which we have referred says: "At one o'clock on Sabbath morning, without a struggle or a groan, he breathed his last. In the most tender manner possible, we shrowded him. Early in the morning I informed his company of his death and every arrangement was made to forward his remains to you. I sincerely sympathize with you in the loss of your dear boys. May God bless and more than sustain you."

Thus, while ministering to the bodily wants of this youthful soldier, he was permitted to soothe with the consolations of the Gospel one who might otherwise have died in the loneliness of the hospital with none to point him to the Redeemer of sinners.

We now resume our extracts from Mr. P's. diary. The entries again become brief and hurried, making a simple record of the events and labors of the day:

"**JUNE 4th.**—Lord, bless me and all thy people to day. Guide our rulers, our officers and soldiers. Be our God. Let not our enemies have dominion over us, I pray thee. Enjoyed the day much in my study. Drilled several hours this afternoon—was quite tired but enjoyed it. Everything is warlike.

11th.—Walked to the church. Front gable nearly done. Lord, I thank Thee for this, and will trust Thee for the rest.

13th.—National Fast day. Lord be with the Southern people to day. Have mercy on our enemies. Quite a good congregation. Read portions of the Scripture, Joel ii; Jonah iii; Matt vi. Services solemn. All attentive. I urged confession of sin, supplication for the mercy of God. Gave many reasons why

19th.— . . . . In my study. O, it is so difficult to read the war news and be devotional. Lord help me.

JULY 7th.— . . . How sad to think of our country's condition. God be merciful to us. Delightful singing. Large congregation. Many soldiers. Communion. Delightful.

8th.— . . . . Selected all my pamphlets. Magazines, addresses, &c. in order to give to the soldiers. . . .

30th.—Went to the new church—upon the tower, &c. The doors and windows are being closed and the lumber piled. . . .

SEP. 8th.—One of the lovliest of mornings. Surely there will be no battle to-day! Gracious God, help our rulers to think of the present and future. * * Opened Sabbath school. Preached to a good congregation—again at 5, P.M. Enjoyed the services more than usual.

17th.—In my study, reading 'McCosh.' I have enjoyed unusual pleasure to day. O that I may have a right appreciation of my privileges and responsibilities.

OCT. 2nd.— ...Took a basket of tracts and pamphlets, &c., went to one of the camps. The men were eager for the tracts, &c. Spent several hours very pleasantly with the officers and men.

6th.— ...R. and I went to the hospital, many sick, but they seemed cheerful. Went to Sabbath school. Preached from Isa. iv: 8-11. Many soldiers present...

Having returned from the Eastern Association sick, he writes:

"**12th.**—This was a sick day, but I felt so thankful that I was at home on a good soft bed, receiving the attentions of my wife, sister and dear children. But I felt especially thankful that the hand of the Lord was in it, controlling everything for my good.

13th.—Beautiful Sabbath morning. The bells rang so sweetly, but I was unable to go out. My wife sat by me and read much, which I enjoyed. Many of the brethren and sisters called in to see me. This was gratifying... A long time since I spent a Sabbath without attending preaching."

The following letters to his daughter may appropriately find a place here, though some of them run into the following year:

WILMINGTON, OCT. 16TH. 1860.

"MY DEAR M.:—We were truly glad this morning to receive your letter which was very interesting and gratifying to us. Your writing shows that by care you will soon excel. I beg of you, my dear, always to take great pains in your writing as well as your other studies. Be sure to act in such a way as to secure the esteem of your teachers and schoolmates. * * * * And now, my dear child, let me affectionately urge upon you the importance of giving your heart to the Saviour. We miss you very much, at prayers, at the table and on all occasions. Dr. Doddridge said to his daughter: 'The most costly thing connected with your education is the separation from you.' So, my dear child, we feel towards you. Your name is often mentioned by us all. Little Georgie says: "Kiss me for Mamie." All join me in much love. From your affectionate father."

Another extract:

"I am truly glad to hear that there is some seriousness in school and that one has made a profession of religion. My dear child, I am much gratified at your progress in your studies, but I feel much more anxiety about your salvation than I do about everything else that concerns you. Do, my child, try and give your heart to Christ. Let me beg you to make it a subject of prayer, that God will enable you to do this now. I should be glad to know how you feel on the subject of religion. Can you not write me? Be sure and read your Bible carefully. Don't allow yourself to become alarmed about the exciting subject now agitating our country. 'The Lord reigneth,' you must look to him for protection." * * * * * *

WILMINGTON, NOV. 29TH, 1860.

"MY DEAR M.:—We were truly glad to get your letter on Tuesday, to see you are so prompt in writing and also to find such manifest improvement in your composition and penmanship. * * * I am much pleased that you are so well satisfied and seem to have so high an appreciation of your advantages. Your privileges are very great, and you must not forget that your responsibilities

*will be correspondingly great. Try and make the most of your advantages. If God shall spare your life, you will live in eventful times—times that will require no ordinary men and women to perform their duties. Try, dear Mary, to be prepared to act well your part, so that the Judge of all will say, 'Well done good and faithful servant, &c.' Cultivate your head and your heart. Ask God to give you a heart to love and obey him. * * * * We have some very nice oranges and bananas. I wish I could send you some. To-day was thanksgiving day, but we observed it as a day of humiliation and prayer to God for our country. Quite a goodly number were out at church. There is little news. We are all well. Often do we think and speak of you and pray for you. All send much love. I am your affectionate father."*

WILMINGTON, DEC. 22ND, 1860.

*"MY DEAR M.:—It would afford us unfeigned pleasure to have you with us on Christmas day, to enjoy your company and that you might also enjoy ours, but I highly approve of the arrangement in not giving vacation in Winter. Since we cannot have you with us, to partake of your usual pleasures with your little brothers and sisters, we propose to send you a little box, as a small token of our remembrance of 'Sis Mary.' Accept of this, my dear child, from us, for all are anxious to assist in fixing up the box. It is a small thing, to be sure, but you will value it not so much for its own sake as for the sake of those who do not forget you in your absence. * * * * * The secession movements are all the talk now. South Carolina is out of the Union. The Lord only knows what is to be the end of all this. * * * * * Let us look to God to preserve our Union, but above all, our souls. Do try, my dear Mary, to give your heart to Christ. All send much love. Your affectionate father."*

WILMINGTON, JAN. 24TH 1861.

"MY DEAR M.—I have been so much engaged of late, that I have not written you for some time. You will not construe this into indifference. I can assure you, my dear child, that you are never forgotten a day, or half a day, by us here. For besides the frequent mention of your name in our conversation, at the family altar, twice every day, the blessing of God is invoked upon our dear absent child. Do you pray for yourself, my dear? I

trust you do. I am glad to hear you speak of your prayer-meetings. Do attend them, Mary: it is a precious privilege, whether it is appreciated or not—for the good are there, but better still, Christ is there! And who would not love to go where Jesus is? It is good to be there. Your letter was received Wednesday morning. We were very glad to get it. I once loved to roam over the same high hills and deep shaded valleys along the banks of the little winding Meherrin. Often have I bowed in prayer in those secluded vales. I frequently walked in the rear of Sister Thompson's house and thence to the river. But I was always alone! and yet not alone, for God, I trust, was often with me, even there. * * * * * We have nothing in the way of news. We have become so accustomed to the most startling things now-a-days, as to count them worthy of but little notice. Such is our nature. Things that would not have been tolerated twenty years ago, are now of every day occurrence and no one is greatly moved by them. * * * * * * * * * * * I want you to exercise your mind in composition as much as your other duties will allow. Take any subject and try to express your ideas upon it, on paper. This is the way persons have been enabled to write for the amusement and instruction of others. Do try and become a good reader. In a word, my dear child, let your profiting be manifest to all, make the best use of your time and distinguished privileges. And do not, I beseech you, neglect to secure the 'pearl of great price'—that inner adornment which adds a lustre and grace to all the rest. See Proverbs iii: 1-26: iv: 5-9. Take these words as coming from a merciful God to you. Believe them, trust in them. * * * I want you to be sure and take much out-door exercise, exert yourself so as to secure physical development. Exercise mind, heart and body. This is the only true development."

WILMINGTON, MARCH 28TH, 1861.

"MY DEAR CHILD:—Your very welcome letter was received on the regular day. We were glad to hear of your continued good health and that you were in the enjoyment of so many and such distinguished privileges. The composition interested us very much. It was very natural, well conceived and happily expressed. I hope you will cultivate a talent for writing—it will greatly improve your taste. Write about real things—things that are lovely, elevating and refining. Describing things or persons is like painting them—they make a deep impression on the mind. A person's character becomes like the objects of his contemplation. How different are

the writings of Cowper and Byron. Both wrote as they thought and felt. An education will be of but little advantage to one who has neither a gift nor talent for conversation or writing. And it will be of less advantage to the world. Then always endeavor to read well, write well and converse well, and while your knowledge will afford you unspeakable pleasure, it will enable you to be both agreeable and profitable to others.

And this is your sixteenth birthday! Can you realize it? It seems but a short time to me since I first pressed you to my bosom as my first-born. God has been very good to you, my dear child. 'The lines have fallen to you in pleasant places and yours has been a goodly heritage' compared with many others. It would have been very pleasant to have you at home to-day, but it will not be long before the end of the session and then we hope to have you with us again. So you must try and be cheerful and the time will soon pass away. We are having pleasant weather. The work on the new church will now go on. We have all been very well. Your little brothers and sisters grow finely and are very interesting to us. You would be greatly delighted with little J., she is so sprightly, and laughs and crows, greatly to the delight of us all. The other children love her very much.

The Lord bless you, my dear M. I am your affectionate father."

WILMINGTON, April 25th, 1861.

"MY DEAR CHILD:—I snatch a moment to drop you a line. I do not think it proper to say much about the all-absorbing topic now, as the papers will tell you all I could. The appearance of our town is greatly changed within two weeks. Then all was active, but now all is dull as to trade. Soldiers are arriving and departing, passing from the South to the North every day. I hope it will not be necessary to dismiss the school. But if your teachers shall judge it best, why, I will make any arrangement that is necessary for your return home. Look up to them as your advisers and they will tell you what is best. God, I am sure, is going to teach us, as a nation, a lesson which his goodness has failed to teach us. And now, my dear Mary, let me, with all the affection of a father, urge upon you the importance of giving yourself to Christ. Let us look to him, not only for our salvation from sin, but also for protection for our persons and our friends, and our dearest interests for time and eternity. Let us not trust in *an arm of flesh, not in armies, or navies, nor in the prowess of man, but in God alone. Our cause is a just one, let us commit it to God, as did our fathers. He defended them and he will defend us. Try and be composed. It is hard for us to get used to the war, but we must learn the lesson. May God preserve you all. I shall not cease to pray for you. Into God's care I commit you. Your affectionate father."*

WILMINGTON, May 2nd, 1861.

"MY DEAR CHILD:—I was truly glad to receive your letter, to learn that you felt willing to remain to the end of the session, but above and beyond all, did I feel glad to hear that some of the girls had found the Saviour precious, and that your heart was interested, and desired that we would pray that you might be a Christian.

Dear Mary, you are the child of many prayers. Your pious mother's, offered while she lived and when she died, stand recorded before the throne of grace pleading for you. And the prayers of your father continually ascend to God for you. But above all, the precious Saviour stands continually pleading for you. But you must also pray; and with confidence you may go to Christ as a sinner. He died for sinners. He came to save the lost. Remember, He is able to save to the uttermost, all that come to God by Him. Repent sincerely; believe in Him, for He is exalted to be a Prince and a Saviour, to give repentance and forgiveness of sins. His blood cleanseth from all sin. Go to him then with confidence. Go, nothing doubting; say 'I must, I can, I do believe.' God bless you, my sweet child, and make you His, to suffer for Him, or do anything. Put all your trust in Him. Your loving father."

WILMINGTON, May 17th, 1861.

"MY DEAR M:—You will perceive that I am again at home, but I have only time to drop you a line, as I shall be very busy preparing for Sunday. I left home on the 8th for Savannah, Ga., where the Convention met on Friday. You will see the proceedings in the RECORDER and I will not give an account of them. The country from Wilmington to Savannah is level and abounds in pines and swamps. Savannah is a beautiful city, having many public squares or miniature parks. There are some beautiful monuments, one to Pulaski, who fell defending the city, Oct. 9th, 1779.

Many of the streets are very wide, having four rows of trees in the middle. There is a magnificent Park and one of the most beautiful Fountains I ever saw. It is in the midst of a circle, and has many devices, beautifully executed; from which jets of water are thrown. Hundreds of men, women and children walk there in the evening. The walks are covered with shells.

When in Charleston, we obtained permission to visit Forts Sumter and Moultrie, and the various places rendered famous in the recent bombardment. Cannon balls and bomb shells are terrible things. Nothing can resist them long. I never could have conceived the terrible destruction, had I not seen it. I brought home some fragments from Fort Sumter, as mementoes. * * * * * *"

EXTRACTS FROM HIS DIARY.

"**JAN. 18th.**—This is one of the darkest mornings we have had, really wintry weather for this climate. O God, bless our brave soldiers in every camp. Came into my study. My little children with me, playing.

FEB. 7th.—Spent some time reading 'Macaulay on History,' and the 'Revolution of 1688, by Sir James Mackintosh.' Was greatly interested in the latter piece, though I had read it before. O, that the Revolution of 1861-62 may be for the glory of God and the progress of mankind.

22nd.—I suppose President Davis is being inaugurated! O God, if it please Thee, own and ratify our government. Give us a name and a place among the nations of the earth.

25th. * * * It is about given up that Nashville has fallen! I don't give it up yet—I will hope against hope. Lord, I look to thee alone. Spent the day in my study, reading Macaulay's History of England. Had a quiet, pleasant time. Sanctify to us the blessings of the day.

MARCH 2nd.—Sabbath. * * * I have spent a most pleasant day. I thank Thee, O Lord, that in the midst of war with man we have peace with Thee.

15th.—Heard the sad tidings to-day, that Newbern had fallen! A stirring day. Captain G's. artillery company, from Mississippi, and Captain B's. passed through town, also Cols. P. and J's regiments. * * * *

APRIL 18th.—Had a most delightful time in my study It was sweet, yea passing sweet, to read and think and write, and thus the time glided away till about 4, P. M. I went to the Hospital and spent the entire afternoon in conversation and prayer with many from North Carolina, Virginia, Georgia, Mississippi, &c.. Some deeply interesting cases.

MAY 12th. ...Letters from Richmond. Great solicitude felt. Lord, deliver our Capitol from our invaders. Went to the new hospital, conversed with all the sick. Found several Baptists, Methodists, &c. Enjoyed talking with them. After resting went to the other hospital and visited all the wards but one and talked with the sick.

18th.—All nature smiles, but O, how dark is the cloud over sinful man. It is just—we have sinned and God has frowned. I preached from 'I will bear the indignation of the Lord, for I have sinned against Him." House crowded. Lord, bless all. Preached again at 4, P. M., congregation good and very attentive.

24th.....Went to hospital—spent a very pleasant time. Find it a delightful work. The sick seem so thankful for Christian sympathy.

29th. . . . At prayer-meeting—no brethren there—quite a goodly number of sisters out. Thank the Lord, they will not forsake their pastor and their Master's cause in the time of trial."

While he was absent from home, attending the regular session of the Ministers and Deacons' Meeting of the Eastern Association, held at Bear Marsh, Duplin county, news came that the seven days' battles around Richmond had commenced. A scene not easily forgotten followed the announcement. Every one present was interested, directly as well as indirectly, in the issue of the conflict. Among the gallant young spirits engaged in the bloody strife was some representative from every family, and the anxiety which pervaded the assembly was painful to witness. Nor was it without cause, as the list of casualties afterwards proved. Mr. P. announced his intention to go to Richmond to aid in caring for the sick and wounded, and the next day found him on his way to the Southern Capitol. A week was spent in the crowded hospitals, in ministering to the sufferers. He writes: "I make it a point to talk to each individual about his soul and ascertain whether he has a hope in Christ. It is interesting to find so large a percentage of pious persons and especially of Baptists. I regard this as one of the most interesting fields for the minister and colporter. I love the work."

And again: "North Carolina has suffered severely in the recent battles. Not less than 3,000 has she lost in killed, wounded and missing. Her devotion to the cause can never be questioned."

About three weeks afterwards he again visited Richmond in charge of a car containing fruits, vegetables and other articles needed for the sick and wounded, sent from Wilmington and other points on the road. The distribution of these articles involved much labor but he cheerfully performed it, feeling that he could not do too much for his country's defenders. Of this trip he writes:

"At almost every station additions were made to the load. I wish you could have seen the quantity at Warsaw, Faison's, Mount Olive and other places. Another car could have been almost filled. All things went on smoothly till we reached Weldon, where the conductor on the Petersburg road refused to take my car. I entreated but it was useless, and there was no alternative but to submit. My car was rolled out from under the shed and as it was now 3 o'clock, A. M., I got into the car and spreading my overcoat on the boxes tried to sleep, but in vain. There were three coops of chickens on board, and as it was early dawn, such a flapping of wings and crowing of roosters you have never heard. It was rather a singular bed-chamber, but far better than many a poor soldier has. They have only the cold, damp ground. They have only hard bread and fat bacon—and sometimes not even that—to eat, while I was in the midst of all sorts of good things. Fruits of the most delicious flavor were around me in great profusion. One comfort I had: it was all for the soldiers.

Soon the Petersburg train came in and the conductor said he would take my car. At Petersburg I delivered the packages for that place, and reaching Richmond about 9, P. M., had to see the car unloaded. It was about 10 o'clock when we got through and I was so tired. The next day I was very busy delivering the packages. The Government sent wagons and hauled them to the hospitals. I expect to spend to-morrow in looking after those persons whom I was requested to find."

His labors in behalf of the soldiers, continued to the close of his life, were highly appreciated by them; and while some on earth have acknowledged him as their spiritual father, doubtless he has already met in the world of bliss many of those to whom he ministered on earth. It is a touching circumstance that among the few present at his burial were several soldiers who thus testified their regard for one who like them offered himself a sacrifice for the good of humanity. In this connection we give a touching testimonial furnished by a soldier after Mr. P's. decease.

"I never knew him well," says the writer, "until the summer before God took him from us. He had come to Richmond on a mission of mercy to the sick and wounded soldiers of North Carolina. It was a work of love and pleasure with him. Being at home wounded, at the time, I was constantly thrown into his company, and never have I seen any man more earnest or conscientious in the discharge of his duty. From early morning till night he was engaged passing from one bedside to another in the various hospitals. Once I urged him to rest. Said he, in reply, 'While I rest this evening, some man may die whom I might tell of Jesus. No, I must work.'

"What most won my admiration and love was his childlike ways and simplicity of heart. His thoughts and actions were alike pure and unselfish. Utter self-abnegation was to be read in everything he did. How hard it seems that such a noble spirit could not be permitted to warm and brighten this cold, unfeeling atmosphere of society below.

"His veneration and love for the soldiers—the private soldiers—were very great. I remember that, in a crowded car between Petersburg and Weldon, he voluntarily gave his seat to a soldier, apparently stronger and in better health than he, and stood the whole way, saying 'the poor fellows need rest more than I do.'

"In 1862 I stood with him on the shell covered beach at Fort Caswell, N. C. The surf was rolling heavily in, and wave after wave broke at our feet. He stood in deep thought, looking out on the vast expanse, for some minutes, and presently exclaimed: 'Life is like those restless billows. O for peace, for rest in Jesus!' His prayer for peace has been answered. Now in the presence of Jesus,

'Not a wave of trouble rolls,
Across his peaceful breast.'"

CHAPTER VIII.

BLOCKADE-RUNNING VESSELS—INTRODUCTION OF YELLOW
FEVER—GREAT CONSTERNATION—REMOVAL OF FAMILIES—
DEATH OF REV. ROBERT DRANE, D. D.—DR. DICKSON AND
OTHER PROMINENT CITIZENS—MEDICAL AID AND SUPPLIES
FURNISHED—REMARKABLE BEAUTY OF THE WEATHER—MR.
PRICHARD'S SELF-DENYING TOILS—HIS CONGREGATION
SCATTERED—SENSE OF LONELINESS—LETTERS.

The blockade of the Southern ports, at the beginning of the late war,
threw the people of those States on their own resources, and some
time elapsed before their energies were directed to a revival of
commerce. Indeed it was not until their necessities became so urgent as to
drive them abroad for such of the *materiel* of war as they could not
produce, and without which their struggle for independence must cease,
that their efforts were turned in this direction. Private speculation, with the
certainty of enormous gains, aided this movement. The summer of 1862
saw the Confederate Government preparing to go largely into the business
of blockade-running. Such capitalists as John Fraser & Co., of Charleston,

with their world-wide credit, had already broken ground and were bringing rich cargoes—munitions of war and the prime necessities of life—into all the ports not then in possession of the Federal forces. But this business, which was lightly considered of such inestimable benefit to the cause and the people at large, was about to strike a heavy blow at the community of Wilmington—a blow unequalled, in its shocking severity, by any of the bloody campaigns participated in by the sons of that city.

In July, 1862, the dashing little *Kate,* formerly a Charleston packet-boat, steamed boldly through the Federal fleet blockading the mouth of the Cape Fear River, and brought up to the wharves of Wilmington a valuable cargo from Nassau, N. P. She rapidly unloaded, as rapidly reloaded with cotton, and departed on her second voyage. But she left behind her that which brought to Wilmington many a sad day, and before which even the horrors and excitement of a great war were forgotten. She left behind her the seeds of the dreadful scourge, the yellow fever.

It did not spread at first—was not acknowledged by the physicians—was not even suspected by the mass of the people. Still it crept insidiously about among the habitations of the poor and amidst the urlieus of the wretched. An uneasy feeling at length began to prevail. There was a singular increase of certain types of fever—a continually increasing mortality in the physicians' lists, until at the end of August people began to enquire into the causes. Still the idea of yellow fever in Wilmington was ridiculed—it was simply absurd.

Thus time wore on, the uneasiness growing, the mortality increasing until the 13th of September, when the point was conceded, and on the 17th Dr. Dickson, one of the leading physicians of the city and himself soon to become one of the victims, reported five cases treated by him. Two days later he reported three more cases, making eight, of whom six died. The way being opened, the physicians began their regular reports, and in a week twenty-six cases and nine deaths were given as the total. With the acknowledgment of the disease and the dread confirmation of those dim forebodings which had made the community restless for weeks, one of those senseless panics, which every one can argue away and so few withstand, set in, and all who were able to get away left at once. For several days the railroads and the high-ways leading from the city were crowded with families seeking safety in flight. This increased the anxiety and alarm of those who remained. The weather was very warm and rain set in. Aided by these causes the disease spread rapidly, and for the week ending October 3rd, 267 cases and 82 deaths were reported. The following week there were 395 cases and 40 deaths. This falling off in the mortality led the people to believe that the disease had culminated; but their hopes were rudely dashed to the ground when the following week footed up 431 cases and 102 deaths, and the week after, 194 cases and 111 deaths. Here the pestilence seemed to have spent its force and rapidly declined: the next week to 116 cases and 40 deaths; then to 47 cases and 30 deaths; then to 21 cases and 21 deaths; the number constantly growing smaller till the fever disappeared.

These statistics include only the white persons who died in Wilmington. Many who fled, bore the seeds of the disease with them to their places of refuge and there died. The negroes were spared at first, almost universally, but towards the close the mortality was greater among them than among the whites. About 150 deaths of blacks are reported.

Thirty-seven per cent of the cases resulted fatally. The mortality was also greater, but the number of cases smaller, in cool weather, while warm weather favored the spread of the disease but moderated its virulence. As in all epidemics the fatality was greater at the beginning and the close.

Among those who perished in this memorable season, besides Mr. Prichard, were, Rev. Robert B. Drane, D. D., rector of St. James (Prot. Epis.) church; Dr. James H. Dickson, one of the most eminent surgeons of the State and President of the N. C. Medical Society, a man beloved by the whole community; Dr. T. C. Worth, brother of our present Governor, one of the leading merchants of the place, admired by all for his hearty energy and genial manners; James S. Green, Treasurer of the W. and W. R. R., the perfect type of the Cape Fear gentleman, one whose large heart embraced all mankind, and whose gentle, cordial charities endeared him to everybody; Col. James T. Miller, chairman of the County court, a polished gentleman and a rough but true friend;—these and many others whose loss, humanly speaking, was irreparable, were swept off in that carnival of death. Every family deplored the fall of some of its members or connections. In some instances whole families were stricken down and followed each other in rapid succession to the city of the dead.

As we have stated above, nearly all who were able to leave the city did so, soon after the prevalence of the epidemic was known. This necessitated the closing of many places of business, and as the stock of provisions in the city, already small by reason of the exhausting demands of the army grew smaller and smaller, the distress among the poor and even among those who were able to purchase, became alarming. No carts laden with the good gifts of the country came to the beleaguered city. Every one shunned it as a doomed place, and it seemed that the horrors of famine were to be added to those of pestilence. Experienced nurses, attendants and physicians were also sadly needed, as the burden of those who remained in the city and were not stricken down, became almost insupportable.

Gen. Beauregard was then at Charleston, in command of a department which embraced the infected district. He was rapidly rising to the zenith of his reputation, and, admired by all his countrymen, was especially the idol[illegible text] those immediately about him. When the condition of the smitten city was made known to him, he at once detailed Dr. Chopin of his staff, to go to its relief. Through his efforts other experienced physicians and a number of skilful nurses soon followed.

In answer to an appeal for provisions, supplies came in from the villages and towns of our own State and from Richmond, Charleston and other Southern cities. A charitable association was formed under the direction of the Mayor, Hon. John Dawson, and when these various energies were concentrated and put in motion, destitution disappeared and the struggle between the belligerents became less unequal.

Thus briefly have we sketched the ravages of the yellow fever in Wilmington, but no pen can adequately picture the utter desolation and loneliness of the place, as the weary days "dragged their slow length along." The weather, much of the time, was beautiful. Said one who was there through it all:

"For days and days the sun has risen in a sky as clear as ever overhung the shores of Italy—'Deeply, darkly, beautifully blue'—and has poured down his rays with a power and splendor that might well entitle our climate to be called a 'sunny' one. And the evening has settled down mild and dewy, as calm and as peaceful as though war, pestilence and famine were unknown. Even the flowers, neglected and run wild, as they too often are in the gardens of deserted houses, are in the fullest bloom, and no leaf falls yet. The trees are green—there is little sign of decay. To-day the sun came out without a cloud and bids fair to continue so. The sky is really beautiful, but it is a fatal beauty, or at least it seems so to us, who know that yesterday over sixty persons sickened, and that of these a number must die. Who know that now, out of our thinned population, some four hundred must be sick with a fearful epidemic. It will be long before any of us who have seen this October through in Wilmington, will take pleasure in the splendors of autumn weather, rivalling the more seasonable glories of summer."

How striking the contrast between this beauty of earth and sky, and the gloom and desolation which brooded over the hearts and homes and avocations of men. The ordinary pursuits of pleasure and gain were forgotten. The streets, deserted by pedestrians, echoed only to the quick rattle of the doctor's buggy or the solemn rumble of the hearse.

In this scene of fear and anxiety and suffering, we need not say that Mr. Prichard was no laggard. At such a time and in such a place, no one was more at home than he. His active sympathies everywhere suggested what was best to be done, and his hands were skilful to prepare what his heart suggested.

On the 12th of August he had parted with his wife and four younger children who were about to visit relations in Richmond, Va., little thinking that he would never meet them again on earth. He continued in the diligent discharge of his duties, visiting the soldiers in the hospital and at the depot, and preaching on the Sabbath to large crowds till his congregations were scattered and broken up by the pestilence. The last Thursday evening prayer-meeting was attended only by him and two faithful female members of the church. Their next meeting was where "congregations ne'er break up" and prayer is turned into praise. In short time they had all passed away from the earth.

When it was ascertained that the pestilence was at work in the place he did not advise others to remain. But he quickly decided that home was his place, and there was no faltering or hesitating after this. Those who knew his social disposition will appreciate the feeling of loneliness which crept over him as one and another of his brethren left. "Sister C. moving away!" This brief entry in his journal notes his sadness at the departure of one who, in seasons of affliction, had always been a ministering angel in her pastor's family. But he was not the man, and this was not the time, to indulge in idle despondency or grief. The suffering ones all about him were crying for relief and he was soon at work like an angel of mercy. His views and feelings and labors at this time are touchingly set forth in his letters to his family.

Before the letters are introduced which refer to the fever, a communication written to his four little children the oldest of whom was nine years old, will be given as illustrative of the tender interest he took in their welfare:

"*MY DEAR CHILDREN, ANNIE, JOHNNIE, GEORGIE AND LITTLE SIS JANIE:—I wonder what you are all doing this morning. If it has been raining in R. as it has been here, I expect you are all in the house—Annie nursing little sissie, and Johnnie and Georgie looking at the books and pictures and playing with little cousin J. I am so glad you are having such a nice time, walking, riding and visiting your cousins and seeing so many interesting things. And you went down to the Capitol Square, and saw the great horse rearing upon the top of the monument. Did you see those men standing below the horse? I want you to tell me their names when you come home, and to tell me what they seem to be doing, &c. Did you see Henry Clay? and the water spouting up and raining down, and the beautiful walks and trees? O, is it not a beautiful place to play in? Did Mama show you the Governor's House? Did she take you into the State Library and show you the large flags and beautiful banners and muskets and swords? You must see them all, and tell me about them.*

"And you went to see dear little cousins' graves. Now, you see, little children die everywhere. O, you don't know how much Papa does miss you. One night last week—Auntie and Bobby were away and I was left all alone. O it was so still! Papa had to to read and have prayers alone! But you may be sure I thought of my darling children and prayed for them and dear Mama, and all our friends. 'I hope you will be very good children. I was very glad to get dear little G's. letter. It his first one to Papa. I shall prize it very highly. Is not yot your little sissie a funny little girl, to say 'Buddy Annie?' What does she call cousin J? I suppose Uncles J. and C. are gone before this. I reckon you have had a nice time with Uncle G. How did he get another horse? Did he find his?

You must give a great deal of love to all from Papa. [illegible text] am your affectionate father."

LETTER TO HIS DAUGHTER AT SCHOOL IN SOUTH CAROLINA.

SEPTEMBER, 16TH, 1862.

"*I am truly glad that the school is so liberally patronized and that everything moves on so harmoniously. My earnest prayer is that the school may be blessed with a gracious revival of religion, and that you, and E., and B., and indeed all the daughters who are there may become the happy subjects of it. I have made this a special subject of prayer. Think seriously of this, my dear child. Without an interest in Christ, all else is nothing and vanity. Without it, all your advantages, intellectual and religious, so far from proving blessings, will turn out to be curses. But possessed of religion all these advantages will turn out to be bright jewels, to adorn and make you useful here and happy hereafter. O, then, seek 'the pearl of great price,' and seek it now! * * * There has been much sickness here for the last fortnight and it is now pronounced yellow fever, by the physicians. There is great excitement. Wilmington has never appeared so desolate since we have lived here. I am truly glad you are so far removed from these sad scenes. The hand of God is in all these things. I feel just as safe here as anywhere else. I could get no nearer to God, except He should take me to Himself, where there is no war and no sickness. My times are in his hands. I would not have it otherwise.*"

(TO THE SAME.)

OCTOBER 1ST, 1862.

.... "*Your aunt and R. and I have all been well thus far, but sickness and death have been and still are all around us. We are in the midst of death. I attended the funeral of one of the first who died of fever, not knowing it at the time, and ever since have been in the midst of it. Our once happy town is almost depopulated. Many have died and a great many have left. It is impossible to give you an adequate idea of the desolate scene you witness at every turn. Many physicians and nurses have been sent from Charleston, for which we feel truly thankful. All will be done that can be, but our trust is in God alone, for He alone can help us and deliver us from this dire calamity. My trust is in Him and to His merciful care and protection I commit you and all my dear family. O Mary, my dear child, let me with all the entreaty of a fond father, beg of you to seek an interest in Jesus Christ. My heart is set on you and all my dear children, to educate you in the way of holiness and usefulness here, and for happiness hereafter. But we know not what God may see proper to do with us. I still hope to see you at the end of this session, but we know not what a day may bring forth. Try and be calm and trust in God, that He will take care of us who are so much exposed. God is with us and can shield us here as well as anywhere else."* * * *

(TO THE SAME.)

OCT. 8th.

"........*We are thus far well, through mercy, but I cannot tell how long we may continue so. Try, my dear child, to realize the true state of things. The Lord will hear us pray to Him. Should I die, I trust I have given my heart to Christ, and that I should go to meet your sainted mother and dear little brother Jemmie. But I trust, my dear child, that God will spare us to meet again in our humble home, to thank and praise him for his loving kindness. And O, Mary, if I could only be permitted to embrace you as a true child of God, my gratitude and joy would know no bounds. I have consecrated you and all the dear children to the precious Saviour."*

* * * * * * * *

(TO THE SAME.)

OCTOBER, 15TH.

"........*Dr. Drane died yesterday. O, how much he will be missed by his people. But God knows best what to do. 'The Judge of all the earth' will do right! My dear child, I have but little time to write you now. My whole time is taken up with trying to do what I can for others. A. (a servant) was taken with the fever last Friday, but is now better. L. (another servant) was taken this morning, so you can imagine our condition.* * * * *Now, my dear, you see on how slender a thread, hang our lives. The Lord alone can keep us or prepare us for affliction or death. Let me urge you, with all a fond father's love, to try and give your heart to the precious Saviour. Why should you delay? By delaying all may be lost. I have recently felt unusual solicitude for your conversion and Robert's. O, if I* *could only feel that you were truly the children of God I should be relieved of a great burden. Do tell me, my dear child, how you feel on this subject."*

(TO HIS WIFE.)

WILMINGTON, Sept. 15th, 1862.

"* * * * *At 3, P. M., Monday, I attended the funeral of Mrs. C., just as a heavy storm of wind and rain commenced, and immediately afterwards I went to mail your letter and got almost wet. It was the heaviest rain I almost ever saw, accompanied by severe thunder and lightning. It tore the streets and roads badly. Wednesday morning I attended the funeral of a child near Kidder's brick-yard. Thursday, most of the day at home. Hearing that the 56th Regt. was up, I started to see them. There is a company of our Camden friends in it, but they had not come up from the Sound. We had a pleasant prayer-meeting in the afternoon—more out than usual. Friday, went to see 56th Regt., met several Camden men—all glad to see me—called to see brother M., brother P. and E. B., all sick. At home till after tea. E. B. died at 6, P. M. I went round there a while, Saturday morning. At 3, P. M., attended E's. funeral, and at 6 attended the funeral of M. S. over the Rail road. And now it began to be rumored that yellow fever was in town, and at a consultation of the doctors, Saturday evening, it was agreed that it was really yellow fever! So I have been in the midst of it without knowing it. Mrs. C's. disease is said to have been the same—there have been nearly a dozen cases, and others are reported to day. Many families are leaving.*

I hear that the Provost Marshal granted passes to over a hundred families yesterday. Yesterday I preached twice, held church meeting, appointed delegates to our Association, took collection for colportage, also called to see a sick lady. I have been to see brother M. this morning. He is better and will leave to-morrow. Black columns of smoke are rising all over the town from burning rosin. I have tried to commit all to God and to feel 'Our times are in his hands.' I have written plainly. I have been much better for some days past and now feel quite well. May God mercifully preserve us all to met again. Let us often be in prayer for each other and our dear family. My kindest regards to all. Love to the dear children from Papa."

(TO THE SAME.)

WILMINGTON, SEPT. 22d, 1862.

"*You don't know how much pleasure your letters gave us. We are beholding a true picture of life. Clouds rest on some, while the sun shines on others. I am glad yours is the sunshine, or 'sunny side,' while ours is 'shady side.' It is all right. God knows what is best, and He will do right. After writing you, on Monday, I remained at home. After tea I was alone, yet not alone, for in heart I was with you and our dear little ones, and my prayer was for God's protecting care over us all. Tuesday many families continued to leave. I spent the day mostly at home reading, &c.*

Wednesday afternoon I went to see a poor, degraded woman who had sent for me. She was dying, but in her right mind. She wanted me to pray with her—I did so—she died that night. I then called to see Mrs. L. and prayed with her, and then went to Mr. G's. On reaching home Mrs. W. had sent for me. I went to the hospital and found a man quite ill, but happy, with whom I conversed. Now, I was tired—the day's work was done. Thursday was a beautiful day. We had services at the usual hour—small number out. I enjoyed the meeting. At 3, P.M., I had a meeting at the Light-House Battery, and at 5, married a couple. * * * Saturday I was sent for to see a man with the fever. I asked Dr. D. what he thought I ought to do. 'Well,' he said, 'I reckon you will have to do as I do. It is like war, we must take our chances. You will have to go and see many during their illness, &c., &c.' It rained in torrents during the day, and Sunday it continued raining all day, until at sunset, it cleared. I preached to very few in the morning. At 9 , I attended the funeral of br other B's child, which died of fever, and at 4, the funeral of a Mrs. B. We had no afternoon services.

I do not think there is any visible abatement in the disease. There have been many deaths—some of other diseases. Two men died just below us Saturday night of yellow fever. It has been showery all day and is raining now—3, P. M. * * * We will write you fully. Don't be alarmed. We are just as near to God here, as we would be anywhere out of Heaven. Let us humble ourselves before God and pray for his protection. I feel calm and resigned. I pray that God will bless you all."

CHAPTER IX.

FEVER STILL RAGING—MR. PRICHARD CONTINUES HIS
ARDUOUS LABORS—CONFIDENCE IN DIVINE SOVEREIGNTY—
LETTERS—ARRESTED BY FEVER—AFFECTING DETAILS—
DEATH—REFLECTIONS.

The city of Wilmington is still wrapped in gloom. All hope of arresting the disease seems now to have passed away, and the comparatively few remaining families are awaiting, with hourly apprehension, its terrible march. Almost every one of these families has been already smitten. They have seen dearly loved ones borne to the grave, or lying prostrate beneath the touch of the pestilence as it swept through the city. How sadly desolate those streets! How mournful the salutation of familiar friends! With what tender sympathy and solicitude these stricken ones clung to each other!

In the midst of this sorrowing population, the subject of this memoir still remained. He could not consent to listen to the yearning pleas of his absent wife and children, as with anxious fear, they were ready to desire his retirement from the post of danger. Gladly would they have shared in the perils of his position, but for his remonstrances and those of others. He could not dare to leave what he believed to be the path of duty. His sensitive heart bled with anguish as he saw his fellow citizens passing away, and heard the lamentations of survivers. For himself he felt no fear. He was ready to live and labor, or to die. The Divine will, he knew, must decide his destiny, and with unfaltering trust he committed himself to God, as unto a faithful Creator.

A moral sublimity appears in this survey. The letter which follows reveals the quiet confidence with which he awaited the return and passage of each day. *"No one thought of God is more precious than that of his sovereignty,"* he writes. That thought was a sustaining power in the midst of his sufferings and toils. Writing to his wife, under date of September 29th, he says:

"This is a most beautiful and lovely morning, contrasting most strikingly with the state of things around us. But who can tell but that it is a cheering omen of the early passing away of the dark death-cloud, that now hangs over our once happy and prosperous town? Thoughts of God have been very precious to me during the prevalence of this disease and our troubles generally, but no one thought of God is more precious to me than that of His Sovereignty. 'The Lord reigneth.' Yes, he reigns in this disease. It is permitted for a most wise and gracious purpose.

"After writing to you last Monday, I attended to considerable business and was quite tired at night, but retired early and slept sweetly. Tuesday, it was manifest that the fever was on the increase, and the people are moving rapidly away. All the drays were hauling rosin, lime, and coal-tar from the gas house. This lime is strongly impregnated with the pungent odor of gas and since it lies at nearly all the doors in town, the whole town smells of gas. Hundred of barrels of rosin have been burnt. I know not whether there is any efficacy in this. It can do no harm.

"Wednesday was truly a gloomy day as to the fever. I attended two funerals, then called at brother T's. and Dr. D's. The Dr. was taken Tuesday, was out till 11, A. M. Went home with a chill. About four I called over to Mr S's. Mrs. S. had just died! Thursday morning I attended the funeral of a child and at 1 1-2, P. M., attended Mrs. S's. funeral and went to the Cemetery. Friday afternoon I attended the funeral of Mrs. H. and also the funeral of an old man, born in 1785. Then made several calls. Saturday visited several sick families, heard of a number of deaths. Dr. Choppin of Beauregard's staff arrived—heard Dr. Dickson was dying, had

made his will, &c. After dinner, sister made soup and I carried it to brother T's. They were so thankful. Sunday morning again went to brother T's and Mr. P's. Mr. G., Mrs. B. and Dr. D. dead; in all I heard from 9 to 12 dead. At 10, A. M., attended Mrs. D's. funeral; went to brother B's. and Mrs. G's. The latter almost dead! Held a short service in the church, and at 1 attended the funeral of Mr. N., and at 4 went to Dr. Dicksons' funeral—no lady with Mrs. D. Dr. Drane and I rode to the Cemetery, and some four or five other gentlemen, also Mrs. D. From his grave went to Mr. G's., and home at sun set. 'In deaths oft.' So you can imagine somewhat only of the state of things around us. It is no longer the Wilmington you left. But the Lord is with us and still will be. When I went down town this morning I saw several from the Sound. Mr. J. died there yesterday of yellow fever. Met Mr. M. from Charleston who is here to aid us in nursing, several nurses have arrived. I have heard of several deaths this morning, several others expected to die. Have attended one funeral and expect to attend another at 4, P. M. You can not conceive of the desolation of our town. Scarcely a store open. We find that many who have left have died. It is thought that it is safer to remain than to leave. I cannot reconcile it to myself to leave the many who must suffer, if some one does not attend to them. I try to be much in prayer. Dr. D. will remain. Mr. R. is here. The Catholic Priest is here, no other ministers. I have thought much of brother H. remaining in Portsmouth. No one would have blamed him for remaining if he had died. On the other hand every body praised him for his devotion at such a time. His conduct and that of other ministers has received the approbation of all.

"Let no one think me reckless of life, or regardless of my wife and children. No indeed, I yield to none in my love of life or of my family. But must a minister fly from disease and danger and leave poor people to suffer for want of attention? How can he more appropriately die, than when facing disease and death for Christ's sake? Did the Saviour ever draw back? I know not what will be my fate. I have committed myself and family to God, praying Him to take care of us all. And if I fall, I leave you to his merciful care and protection. I think much of you. I took a mournful pleasure, yesterday, in looking at all the daguerreotypes. My heart was moved. Some here, and some have crossed the river and are happy. How soon others may go, God only knows. Are we prepared for it? I feel deeply for M. and R. Do all of you unite in prayer for their salvation and the servants also. I speak of them, for they are older. Tell your father, I thank

him for his kind words. They are such as I have always received from him. I will try and write him ere long. He will still be your father and the father of our dear little ones, if I shall see them no more. But I expect to see you all again on earth. I desire to be affectionately remembered to every one of the family. Kiss the sweet children for Papa."

It was not the will of God that his hopes should be realized. His beloved family was to be seen no more on earth. But every day he was waiting for the summons of his Divine Master. The details of the communication which follows, are peculiarly affecting, giving a view of the sickening horrors of the position, and illustrating the sublime heroism of this servant of Jesus, as well as the faith and hope which so triumphantly bore him along the pathway of danger. He writes to his family, October 5th:

*"Notwithstanding it is Sunday, I conclude that it will not be displeasing to God for me to write you. And what a great privilege I esteem it, to be permitted again to let you know of our welfare. Through the abounding mercy of God we are all spared and well thus far. I will give you a running sketch of each day since I last wrote. Mr. Wm. H. died on Tuesday morning. The same day I attended the funeral of brother B. and his little babe—three of this family are gone. At 2, P.M., attended the funeral of a little boy living near us. * * * Wednesday was a most beautiful day. . . . Went for medicine for Mr. T., who has the fever, also Mrs. P., her mother and little J. So you see it is around us and even at our door. In the afternoon I went to see J. P., who has the fever, and also to brother H's., then to brother T's, Mr. P's. and home. Thursday, at 10, A. M., I went to attend the funeral of Mrs. K's daughter, thence on by brother T's. and bought some things for them. I had a distressing headache much of the day. Mr. M. sent a barrel of flour, of the Gallego brand, for us to distribute among the poor. We sent some to —, and I carried some to sister S. We have no prayer-meeting on Thursday afternoon now. There is no one to go. Dr. D. is very agreeable—consults freely with me, and is acting nobly and doing all he can. So also is Father M. very sociable. I met him the other evening and he introduced me to another Priest from Charleston, who came with the 'Sisters of Mercy' to nurse.*

FRIDAY.—*I slept sweetly last night, and this morning my head is entirely easy. It is somewhat cloudy. I do not go out till 8, or 9, A. M. Just as I was* *going down sister S. sent for me. I went, found Mr. S. dying! He died a little after 9. As you may suppose, sister S. was crushed. At 10, A. M., attended the funeral of old Mrs. S. In the afternoon went to see Mr. S., who has the fever. It was his mother who died. Attended another funeral at 11, A. M. After tea went for medicine for Mr. P. Poor fellow, I pity him, he has to do everything. And poor Mrs. T. has no one to aid her, except what we do. She seems very thankful. I am glad we can do anything for anybody. * * * This, Sunday morning, we had services in our church—a dozen or more whites and as many colored persons present. I spoke from Jno. iii: 35. The morning was beautiful, but very warm. Just as we were going to church, I perceived that the wind had shifted from South to Northwest. It was a little cooler. About 2 it began to cloud up and at 3, P. M., the wind changed to Northeast, and whilst I have been writing this, in my study, we have had thunder and lightning, and a heavy shower. I feel confident God will do all things well. Indeed I find no comfort, only as I am enabled to trust him implicitly. We are so prone to think that some other way than His way is best. I feel constant need of correcting myself. But I do find it sweet to bring my mind to feel that 'His Kingdom ruleth over all,' and that 'He is head over all things to the church,' and that the 'Father has committed all things into His hands.' Now, if the Father has committed all his vast concerns to Him, can we not commit ourselves and all that's dear to us, to Him? Surely, we can, we will. But this resignation, so far from causing us to feel indifferent or to relax our exertions, is our only encouragement to feel interested and to put forth all possible effort. * * * **

"O, yes, we thought of darling little J's. birthday. God bless the dear children, and dear mama, and all. O, He has greatly blessed us. 'Shall we receive good at the hand of the Lord and not evil?' We must not expect an uninterrupted course of enjoyment in this world. And if we are all spared through this time of great affliction, there is assuredly a day ahead of us that will fill us with sorrow and mourning. I reckon, if Lazarus could have been consulted, he would rather not have been raised from the dead. 'To die is gain' to the christian. I often think of John Foster's consoling words to Miss Sarah Saunders: 'But if He, who is the sovereign and gracious Disposer of our life and all our interests, has determined otherwise, it is, indeed, Miss Sarah, it is because that will be better: and you yourself will know and pronounce it to be better. Oh, it is better be a happy and immortal being in the presence and enjoyment of the infinite good and mingling in the society of angelic spirits and of the 'spirits of the

just' that are already associated with them, than to stay in this world, in even the happiest lot that Providence ever allots to the most favored of mortals. To make a complete, final, triumphant escape from all the evils of our degraded and afflicted nature and this melancholy world; to be clearly and forever beyond the region, and beyond all possibility of sin and sorrow—this is worth resigning all on earth to attain.'

"It matters but little when, where or how we die, so we are prepared for it. Let us strive for it. I trust, my dear wife, you will try and be calm and trustful. I sincerely pray we may all meet again on earth. No one's family is dearer to him than mine is to me. I thank God for what he has permitted us all to enjoy together—few families have enjoyed more. I am conscious of many, very many imperfections and weaknesses. No one regrets it so much as I do. O, that I were freer—yea, entirely free from all imperfections and a more lovable man than I am. Through abounding grace I trust to be made clean and pure and holy, not having 'spot or wrinkle, or any such thing.' * * * We have had a fine shower. It is 4, P. M., and yet cloudy. Sincerest love to all. Kiss the dear children for papa."

A few days pass away, all filled up with pains-taking endeavors to soothe the bereaved and to nurse the sick. Under date of October 12th, he again writes to his anxious wife:

"We were glad to get your letters this morning, informing us that you were all well and enjoying so many privileges. It is such a comfort to us to know that whatever may be our lot, the lines have fallen to you in goodly places. It would add much to our already great affliction, to hear that any of you were sick. God, I trust and believe, will take care of you all. Another week has passed away since I wrote you, and still, through mercy, we are yet spared. On going down to mail my last letter to you I found that Mr. S. was dead! And just as I got home, about 5, Mrs. P. died! It was, indeed, a gloomy afternoon to us. Monday morning I called to see Mrs. Dr. D. She was so glad to see me. She was calm but deeply afflicted. She called in the servants and asked me to have prayer. I did so. I then went to see poor E. It was truly affecting to hear her lamentations. I tried to comfort her. Went to brother T's.—he is better. Called to see a brother P., very ill of fever. He died on Tuesday. I was sent for to see a poor woman dying, and went. That afternoon brother W. was taken sick of fever. Tuesday, I carried refreshments to brother T. They were so thankful. Old

*Mr. M. came for me to see his wife—she was dying. It was a truly affecting scene. They had lived so long together. She died that night. Col. M. died to-day. He will be much missed in our town and county. Wednesday, called to see brother W.—he was doing well. Sister P. had sent for me—I went, prayed and conversed with her. * * * At 4, P. M., I attended the funeral of Mrs. M., and called to see sister S.—she is deeply afflicted. After going to the office went to see brother W.—heard that Mrs. D. was taken sick Tuesday. Thursday, remained at home most of the day. After tea brother B. came for me to attend the funeral of brother D. to-morrow early—had not heard a word of his illness. Friday at 8, A. M., attended brother D's funeral, and at 10, went to poor little S's. funeral. Mr. D. is getting better. Heard to-day that Dr. D. was sick. Called to see brother T's. family—they are improving. Called to see old Mr. M.—very sick. Also sister S.—her baby is sick but better. While at dinner sister H. sent for me—that the Dr. was dying. I hastened there. He died at 2, P. M., and his sister was also dying. I helped to shroud the Dr. Miss S. died a little after midnight—both dead in the house at the same time! This is affliction indeed! You cannot conceive the state of things we are in. The Lord deliver you, I pray, from ever experiencing it. You can scarcely get any one to help shroud and bury the dead. Miss S. had a female nurse from Charleston, the Dr. had none— he was only taken Tuesday night. All Mrs. H's. servants but one have had the fever. She is now alone!*

"*This, Sunday morning, it was raining quite hard. At 9, A. M., I went to bury Dr.—one gentleman went with me—it rained all the time. I desired to bury them both in one grave, but we could not get Miss S's. coffin in time, so at 2, P. M., I went alone to bury Miss S. I rode both times in the Dr's rockaway. So father, son and aunt sleep together. Mrs. H. has no one here to look to but me. I feel sorry for her.*

"*We have had no services to-day in any of the churches. Surely there never was a darker day in Wilmington than this has been. The Lord only knows what is in the future for us. To Him, I desire to commit all. It is now getting late and I am tired, so good night.*

Monday, 11, A. M. Attended a funeral at 9. I hear of a great many new cases this morning. Not a drugstore open. They will try and get some apothecary from Charleston. It is still cloudy and showery. And now, I again commit you and the dear children to our merciful Father. Tell the dear children 'Papa often thinks of them, and prays for them, and hopes to see them again. I want them to be good children and mind mama.' A great deal of love to all. Let us continue to pray for one another. God bless you all.”

Two days later, and his last letter is begun. It narrates the details of the overwhelming trial which was upon him, in witnessing the increasing number of cases of sickness and death. It would seem to have been a miracle, if his sensitive nature had not yielded to the pressure which was upon him. Tenantless homes were all around, and those which were occupied presented only scenes of suffering and lamentation. At length his own home is invaded by the pestilence. His servants and his sister are stricken, and then the premonitions of fever are felt in his own person. All these are noted with an affecting particularity in the letter which follows. The worst apprehensions of his absent and agonized family were about to be realized. He who was so deeply loved, and who had been so eminently their guide and support, was to be taken from them. The communication, dated Oct. 17th, fell with crushing weight upon their spirits, and gladly would they have rushed to soothe his dying moments. It is here given:

“Though it is only Friday morning, I conclude to commence my weekly letter to you. I did not go on the street till after dinner, Monday, then heard that Mr. McR., of the Commercial bank, was dead, that sister H. had the fever and Dr. Drane also was ill. I called to see Sister H. It was very damp and cool. Tuesday, at 12, I attended the funeral of Mr. M.; at 1 that of our brother K.; and at 2 that of Mrs. B. who lived near us, mother of that little boy who always seemed so glad to see us. Poor little fellow, at the funeral, he cried as if his heart would break, ‘O mama! my Mama!’ And poor Mrs. K. is heart-broken. She has two little children. Old Mr. M. is thought to be better. To-day I called at Mrs. D’s., she is also better; thence to see sister S. They are all better there; then to brother T’s., they are up and much better. Their little servant boy died Saturday. From there I went to Mrs. K’s.; the remains had just been carried to the grave without any minister being there; the family all sick—then to sister H’s. and inquired for Dr. D., no better. Wednesday, our other servant was taken sick. Dr. C. came to see her. Heard that Dr. Drane died last night, also Mr. H. and Mr. N.! Brother H. sent for me, has the fever. Called on Mr. C. He and his wife both in bed. The children have had the fever and are up; another lady sick with fever, with them; I prayed with them; they seemed so glad I called. At 3, P. M., I attended Dr. Drane’s funeral. Mr. Terry read

*the burial service. He looks very badly. He is staying at the sound, but says he is coming up to town next week. I advised him not, he is so feeble. Only two ladies went to the grave, several gentlemen. On my way home from the Cemetery called on sister P. She is well. Thursday. Sister had a chill last night, and is in bed sick! So you see, step by step the fever advances. I went for Dr. C. Sister was very sick all day. I had to do a hundred things and knew not how to do any, but did the best I could. I rested a little while at 4, P. M., then went out and had provisions sent to sister P. On coming home I had our supper and gave the servants theirs. They are both better. About 9 I retired, but was so tired I did not get any sleep, till after 12. Sister is extremely feeble this morning. I made coffee and we had our breakfast; attended to getting dinner. * * * Mr. T. and wife are both better. Mrs. G. better, but L. has black vomit. Six of Dr. S's, family are sick. I have not been out to-day, 1, P. M. I have rested while writing you and soon must commence my evening duties. It is quite clear and pleasant. We know not what a day may bring forth. Look to God.*

*Saturday morning, 9, A. M. O, such a night as my poor sister had; perfect prostration and utter weakness. I sat up some time and did all I could and then went to bed, but not to rest and sleep, but to listen to sister's plaintive moan. I think I heard the clock strike every hour except five. Late last evening I went down to try and hear from brother H., &c.; heard they were improving and that Mr. Q., of the Cemetery, was dead. He helped to bury Dr. H. on Sunday. This morning is quite clear, and cooler. L. G. died at day break this morning and J. is thought to be dying!! I have not heard from the street and shall not go out to to day. Mr. M. will have something cooked for us to day, but the Lord only knows who will eat it. * * *Well, my dear Wife, and do you ask me, how I feel in view of never meeting my loved ones again on earth? I cannot tell you. I must not conceal from you the true state of the case by which we are surrounded. I am sick now. My poor back and head ache, the true symptoms of fever. This is my bodily condition. I have no other trust but the precious Redeemer and He is precious to me. Though it may be feverish excitability, I am not afraid to commit you and my dear six children to Him. He has taken care of me and He will take care of you all. But, O, it is hard to think we cannot wipe the death-damp from each other's brow! Notwithstanding this, I would not have you here on any account. I know every feeling of your heart impels you to share our fate. But think of dear Mrs. Judson and those most beautifully touching lines beginning, "We part on this green* *islet love, &c." They express my present feelings. But I must finish this for R. to mail this evening. I hope to be spared, but in case I should not, I wish to make some suggestions."*

Here follow some arrangements and directions for his family:

"O, I could write a volume! But my history is before the world, and I trust my record is on High. 'I am in a strait, &c.' To God I commit you all, and my spirit I commit to Him. Sweet babes, dear wife, friends and brethren, vain world, adieu! In hope of eternal life."

The hand of the destroyer was upon him as he wrote. He felt it and remarked to one near him, "This is the last letter I shall ever write to my wife." Alas! that his presentiment should so soon have been realized. Always very prudent in his habits, it was hoped that he might escape. Many hearts, far away and in different parts of the country, were deeply solicitous about him, and many prayers were offered up for his safety. About the first of November the Baptist State Convention met at Wake Forest College. During one of the evening sessions of that body, Rev. R. B. Jones, of Hertford, arose and announced that Mr. P. lay dangerously ill at his home in Wilmington and suggested that special prayer be offered for his recovery. A stillness as of death prevailed, as the speaker proceeded, and the petition which followed found a response in every heart. But Mr. P's. work on earth was done. Faithfully had he toiled in the Master's vineyard for more than thirty years, and now the summons had come for him to enter into that eternity of rest for which he had been so long ripening and to which he had so often looked forward with earnest longings.

For several weeks the work of death had been drawing nearer and nearer to his residence, until at last he wrote, as whole families, in houses on every side, were prostrated: "Death all around us. They fall as in battle on our right hand and on our left." Now the disease enters his own household, attacking his servants first, and then his only sister who refusing to be separated from him had cheered his loneliness. Two days after his sister was prostrated, he too, smitten with fever and worn down by anxiety and fatigue, retired to his chamber, never again to leave it on errands of mercy.

The only well person now left in the family was his eldest son who succeeded in securing an excellent nurse and experienced physicians. For two weeks his condition was critical and his sufferings were great. Then the crisis seemed to be past and he was evidently better. His physician pronounced him out of danger. He was able to sit up a while, enjoyed his nourishment and even began to speak of the return of the absent members of his family. But he did not gain strength or improve as rapidly as his friends fondly hoped he would, and an attack of jaundice soon came on. Such was the prostration of his system that he sank rapidly under the new attack.

The details of those days of weariness and watchfulness are affectingly given in letters of the son and sister of the afflicted one:

"MY DEAR MOTHER:—I went to the office this morning and was very glad to find a letter from you, and will answer it immediately. Every one in the house, but myself, is now sick. Pa was taken yesterday morning, though he had a chill the night before. The servants are improving, they can be up a little, though they don't help us much. I was at the store yesterday, when I was sent for, as Papa was taken sick. Capt. E. immediately came here, while I went to get a nurse. Mr. S. the superintendent let me have a very good one, a mulatto man, who nursed at Norfolk and Portsmouth. * * *

"The Journal has suspended at last, on account of sickness of hands, though they issue a bulletin nearly every day, with the most important intelligence; the highest number of cases yet in 24 hours is 87. Tell Johnnie, that Johnnie and Lizzie G. both died yesterday, and while I write, a wagon stands at the door with J's. coffin in it. There has been a scarcity of meat here; the country carts have stopped coming in altogether, but with the contributions, which have been very liberal, I suppose there has been no actual suffering. I have seen several dray loads of coffins, from abroad I suppose, going to the depot of supplies, our carpenters not having been able to supply the demand. Dr. C. attends us and he says, of 138 patients, he has lost but two in the last 19 days. Capt. E. says, there is more in the nurse than the Dr., and he says we have a faithful nurse. * * * *The town, as you may imagine, is quite deserted; you scarcely see a vehicle but the hearse and the doctor's buggy!*

"3, P. M. I have just been to Papa's room. He says his medicine has operated finely, and having bathed his feet in salt water, and applied

mustard plasters to his limbs, he is now in a profuse perspiration and pretty comfortable. He says, that, till after midnight, he had a fearful time, suffering very much with his head and back. The Dr. says he is better and doing very well."

WILMINGTON, OCT. 25th, 1862.

"DEAR MAMMA:—*Supposing you would be anxious to hear from us as soon as possible, I will write to-day. Monday Papa was not so sick as he was Tuesday. Wednesday and Thursday he seemed better, but Thursday night and yesterday, he was prostrated by weakness and want of sleep. This morning he seems rather better and stronger, having slept several hours, last night. All who know anything about this disease agree that it brings the patient down faster than any other. Dr. A., who only had a slight attack, said he was so weak, it was positively painful. * * * You need not be uneasy about our having friends. Capt. Ellis, Mr. S. Martin and others have been very kind. * * * I am very glad to say that the disease is abating; yesterday there were only three new cases, but eleven deaths.*

ROBERT."

Here follow extracts from letters from his sister who, amid the feebleness attending a partial recovery, so tenderly watched over and nursed her dear brother in his last days of suffering.

"*Thursday night brother had a dreadful time; did not sleep at all, his mind wandering. Yesterday he was prostrate. I asked the Dr. to tell me what he thought of his case. He said it was extremely critical, but hopes by careful nursing he may be spared. Myers, our nurse, is very kind, does everything I ask him cheerfully. He talks so kindly to brother; I feel thankful we have such a nurse. The Dr. did not feel much encouraged this morning, but Myers thinks him a little stronger. He appears inclined to sleep, but when awake is so feeble he can scarcely talk. Dr. A. made him a friendly call, said he was doing very well, he must have sleep, &c. Brother has been troubled with hiccups since Thursday. Mr. M. and his mother are unbounded in their kindness and often come to see us. The 'Sisters' have been in once. I was glad to see them. They talk so kindly.*

2, P. M. Capt. Ellis thinks brother better this afternoon."

"OCT. 26. This is one of the most dreary Sabbaths I ever saw. The rain poured in torrents till after eleven, then, for an hour, a high east wind; now a steady rain. I hardly know what to say about brother; the Dr. says he does not see much change in him. He is inclined to sleep most of the time, has nothing to say to me to-day; yesterday, he talked to me a good deal. He takes his nourishment, but I am anxious to see him more like himself.

"Capt. Ellis comes in twice a day. We missed him to-day. He is very kind. I shall always love him.

"MONDAY MORNING, Oct. 27th.—Cold and clear, with high wind; almost cold enough for ice, very unfavorable for the sick. O! such an anxious night I had! Though the weather was so piercing, I had to get up in the night and come into brother's room, to see how he was. To-day, I am sitting in brother's room, by a good fire. I feel encouraged about him. The Dr. thinks he has passed the crisis, and says the cold weather will brace him up. O, that our hopes may be realized. Brother certainly appears better to-day, though he says he does not feel any stronger. Yesterday he could scarcely speak to be understood. I felt, when I had written one page, I never would finish this letter, for I feared the scenes of to day would not be such as I could write. I pray that I may feel as humble and thankful as I ought, if my brother is spared. He looked so changed yesterday. He is very yellow. Yesterday he had an unnatural look about the eye, in fact, everything to me was then discouraging, but Myers did not appear discouraged. This morning I sent early into brother's room to see how he was. I heard him answer in my room; how glad I felt to hear his voice. The Dr. thinks there will hardly be many more cases of fever, after this; said Saturday, he had twelve new cases, but none since. If the wind falls to night and unless there is a change in the weather, we will be apt to have a white frost. How glad I should be if brother was only as strong as I am!"

"OCT. 29th.—Thanks to our Heavenly Father, my dear brother is, I hope, much better. He is still very feeble, but says, he enjoys his nourishment. He did not sleep much last night, but said he rested and he had several naps through the day yesterday. I feel very much encouraged. Dr. C. told him

*yesterday he should dismiss him in a few days. Dr. A. called last evening, said all brother's symptoms were very good and he expected to see him up in a few days. You would be shocked to see him now, his skin is so yellow, but his eyes look clearer. * * * If you do not get a letter for several days you need not feel anxious. If any thing happens Capt. E. will let you know."*

*"NOV. 4th.—Brother is still very feeble, indeed he does not appear any stronger than he was a week ago. Though he takes nourishment, he does not gain his strength. He can't sleep at night, but I tell him he sleeps in the day. He says, he dreamed of you last night. When he speaks of getting well, he talks of his desire to see the children and says he shall miss Annie so much if she remains in R., but appears willing she should do so. He says, he had made up his mind he should die, and felt perfectly resigned. I think Dr. Drane's death had a very sad effect on him. They had been together a great deal, before the Dr. was sick, and you know he was a man of very social manners. Brother became more attached to him than ever. Dr. W's. death afflicted him very much, it was so unexpected to us all—I think it was rather too much for brother in his weak state. * * ***

*"Brother tells me to write you just how he is and I try to do so. You must not think I wish to excite your feelings. I did hope by this time he would be able to sit up. Dr. C. has just been in. He had not been in since last Wednesday, said he left brother doing well, and he had been very busy. He says brother has the jaundice, but gives me great encouragement. * * * Two of the 'Sisters of Mercy' have just called. I wish you could see Mother Theresa, she is one of the sweetest looking persons, I ever saw. I do love to have her come. She brought Dr. Corcoran, a Catholic Priest from Charleston, with her one time.' She has been in often." * * ***

*"NOV. 8th. 1862.— * * I hardly know what to say about brother. He had a bad night, last night, suffers much with his back; has not been as well to-day. Dr. C. has gone up the country. Dr. A. came in to-day. He talked very encouragingly, but brother appears discouraged, says he can't live unless he is relieved. Dr. A. is here now, brother told him he felt better. I try to be as cheerful as I can. The nurse leaves to-night, being obliged to look after his family in Charleston, but I can do very well; am glad to have the opportunity to sleep in the room with him, for I can hear him at night and*

wish I was with him. I know what it is, to lie awake so much when every one is asleep. * * *

"*Well, we have had a frost and I do hope the fever will disappear. A great many persons were up from the Sound at night. I do not want you to come too soon. You spoke of hoping soon to get a letter from brother. He has not even read one of your letters yet. You cannot imagine how feeble he is. I feel hopeful, but when he seems so low-spirited, you must know I feel badly. I often wish I could see your Father with his cheerful face. I never saw Capt. E. appear so cheerful.*"

"*SUNDAY, 8, A. M., NOV. 9TH.—Another frost, and ice! Brother had a more comfortable night. The Dr. told me to give him paregoric every hour till it quieted him. Two doses were sufficient and he slept pretty well till four o'clock this morning. He has now had his breakfast and is quiet.*"

The next letter was more startling than previous accounts gave reason to expect. It is from his oldest son:

NOVEMBER, 12TH, 1862.

"*DEAR MAMA:—Knowing you will be anxious to hear from us—I will write a few lines. Since Saturday papa has had a change for the worse, suffering a great deal of pain. Yesterday and last night, he was very sick—indeed I think the Dr. had little hopes of him in the evening. Between nine and ten last night, he was somewhat relieved, and this morning he may be a very little better, but I am afraid not. Yesterday he seemed impressed with the idea that he was dying, but this morning he lies quiet and says little. Mr. W. and Mr. C. sat up with him night before last, and Mr. W. last night. Aunt L. hardly leaves him a moment. Yesterday evening he kept calling for you and would not be pacified till aunt L. came in, who had gone down stairs. I do trust he will be spared, but he is very sick now. We have had three white frosts, and ice a quarter of an inch thick, but the cool weather does not check the fever much. Nine or ten new cases yesterday—the reason of which, it is thought, is, that so many people have come back and taken it almost directly.* * * * *

Your affectionate son."

(FROM CAPTAIN ELLIS.)

NOVEMBER 13TH, 1862.

"DEAR SISTER:—I have just left brother Prichard, and it is with pain I have to announce the Dr. informs me he has no hopes of his recovery. God give grace to bear up under the heavy affliction. I will write by next mail.

Affectionately your brother,

C. D. ELLIS."

(FROM THE SAME.)

NOVEMBER 13TH, 1862.

"DEAR SISTER P.:—I dropped you a line yesterday with promise to write again to-day. Your husband, our dear pastor, is still alive, but I cannot say he is any better. While life lasts there is hope. Our most earnest prayers are going up continually that God will spare him.

Very truly,

C. D. ELLIS."

The hour of his dismission had come. As a few loving ones surrounded him, on the 13th of November, nearly a month after he was taken sick, his spirit entered into rest. His devoted friend and constant attendant, Capt. C. D. Ellis, communicated the sad intelligence to his bereaved wife in the following note:

"It becomes my painful duty to announce the departure of our dear, dear pastor. He left us last night, at half past eleven o'clock, and with a sweet smile on his face, has gone to reap the reward of his works. I am sure, if he could communicate with us, he would say: 'Grieve not for me.' May we not comfort ourselves with the thought that he is now a ministering spirit watching over us? O, that the Lord may give us grace to bear this heavy loss and say, 'Thy will be done.'"

(FROM MISS LYDIA PRICHARD.)

NOVEMBER 14TH, 1863.

"*MY DISTRESSED SISTER:—I feel I cannot sleep to-night without writing to you about my dear brother. How sad and lonely we are! Our friends have done everything they could. All the neighbors have been so kind and seem to feel so deeply. My dear brother would not let me leave him one minute. When he slept a little I would lie down by his side and drop asleep, but waked the moment he stirred. Brother W. staid with us, all the time, from Monday till after all was over. He was so good to brother, lifting him and waiting on him. Brother could not bear him to be absent; but if I told him he was eating or sleeping, he would be satisfied. Other brethren did all they could. * * * * * Oh! how pleasant my dear brother looked after he was dead. Brother W. said he appeared as he did when he was administering the communion. There was a sweet smile on his countenance. * * * I do not think brother wanted you to come home; he never said anything like it to me. Mrs. S. was sitting where he could see her one day—he was suffering very much—he called her to him and said: 'Mrs. S. you are a wife and a mother and you will know how to sympathise with my wife.' The morning he was taken sick he was writing a letter. To a colored woman who came in he said: 'I am sick; I expect this is the last letter I shall ever write to my wife.' I think he was impressed with the idea he should die from the first. Being asked, if he was going to write for you to come home he replied: 'No, I do not want wife to come home.' * * * He was truly patient, during his sickness, never murmuring or complaining at anything. I shall always feel thankful for the privilege of nursing him. He told me to have him buried on the right hand side of dear little Jemmie.*" * * * *

During his sickness he conversed but little except in the few days of his apparent convalescence. Then he enjoyed hearing his sister read the Bible, Jay's Exercises, and occasionally the newspapers. He read himself, with his accustomed interest, a part of the proceedings of the North Carolina Baptist State Convention, as published in the *Biblical Recorder.* This was the only session of that body from which he had been absent since his return to his native State.

About his absent ones he said but little—the subject was too tender to pass his lips. But his letters show that they were ever present to his memory. May we not imagine how his heart yearned towards the loved group in a distant city, and his darling first-born, absent at school? Doubtless many of the lonely hours of those long, wakeful nights were occupied with thoughts of the dear ones whom he was to meet no more on earth. Thoughts too of the flock with which he had labored, and which would now be as sheep without a shepherd, came over him. Knowing him as we do, we seem to hear him exclaim, as he turns from these things to the doctrine of God's sovereignty: "The Lord reigneth."

It was a merciful arrangement of Providence, that he was not stricken down during the early prevalence of the epidemic. After laboring for weeks in behalf of others, administering to their physical and spiritual wants, he was permitted to receive the kind attention of friends, some of whom had but recently recovered from the dreadful disease. He was also permitted to enjoy the tender care of his sister, who was wonderfully strengthened for her labor of love.

So rapid was his decline, and so unexpected his death, that while the absent members of his family were anticipating a speedy reunion around the fireside, and his friends were rejoicing over the tidings of his improved health, a little band of sincere mourners accompanied his remains to their last resting-place and laid him—in the spot selected by himself—by the side of "darling Jemmie," there to repose till the morning of the resurrection.

CHAPTER X.

EXTENSIVE USEFULNESS—VIGOROUS INTELLECT—
RETENTIVE MEMORY—COURAGE—CONFIDENCE IN HIS OWN
JUDGMENT—STRENGTH OF WILL—LITTLE POETIC
IMAGINATION—WARM SYMPATHIES—CONSECRATION—
INTEREST IN WORKS OF BENEVOLENCE—MANNER IN THE
PULPIT—HIS DOMESTIC HABITS—FAMILY WORSHIP—
TOUCHING INCIDENT—ESTIMATE OF CHARACTER BY A
VIRGINIA PASTOR.

Mr. Prichard's character is so fully illustrated in the preceding pages that it is perhaps needless to say more; but the pen lingers as the memory of all that he did and all that he was rises before us. That he was a man of more than ordinary ability is shown by the success which be achieved and the position to which he rose in spite of the most serious disadvantages. "By their fruits ye shall know them," is a rule which is susceptible of application to the intellect as well as the heart. Judged according to this standard Mr. Prichard's talents were of a very high order. Who that saw him in his youth, toiling at his trade, would have anticipated the brilliant and useful career on which he entered a few years afterwards, and which he steadily pursued, rising step by step till the close of his life? All the probabilities were against such a supposition for the poor young man. Few accomplish more even under the most favorable circumstances.

He had a vigorous and active intellect, rather practical than speculative, preferring to take the materials within his reach and fashion them for purposes of usefulness, instead of striking out as a pioneer or adventurer in the the world of thought. On all subjects which engaged his attention his reasoning was rapid yet cautious and accurate. His judgment, when uninfluenced by disturbing causes, was correct. His nervous organism was unusually delicate, and when it was excited or deranged by disease or other causes the careful discrimination, which marked his calmer moments and made him so safe a counsellor, sometimes failed him temporarily. This was especially the case amid the confusion incident to the proceedings of deliberative bodies. At such times he occasionally missed the point under discussion, but pressed his views with force and earnestness till a brief interval of quiet reflection served to show him his mistake.

He had a retentive and ready memory—gathered knowledge from every available source and what he once digested and stored away he could easily recall when the occasion required it. His information, not only on general topics, but also on many which lie beyond the range of ordinary discussion and investigation, was extensive and thorough. Nor was it thrown together promiscuously, as is sometimes the case, like the articles in a lumber room. Order and taste presided over memory and his knowledge was like the armament of a fort under the direction of a skilful commandant, each part brought out at the proper time and used to the best advantage.

Courage, both physical and moral, he possessed in a remarkable degree. The thought of what others would say, of personal popularity or unpopularity, had not a feather's weight in forming his opinions or determining his course of action. The fear of the Lord, of doing wrong and thereby incurring the displeasure of the Master, was the only fear he ever knew. Opinions which he honestly held, no considerations of expediency could keep him from avowing. A course of action which he felt to be right, he steadily pursued, no matter what the opposition which he encountered.

And yet he was neither rash nor reckless. Ordinarily he was prudent, both in word and deed.

As might be expected, from his early experiences and his positive character, he had great confidence in his own judgment. But there was about him no pride of opinion. Always open to conviction and willing to hear both sides, he would urge his own views and plans till convinced that he was in the wrong. Then he never hesitated to make full acknowledgment of his error. In the heat and excitement of debate he was sometimes apparently discourteous—never intentionally so—to others, but when it was made known to him or he had reason to suspect it, he made prompt and ample reparation. One who had much pleasant intercourse with him, furnishes the following incident, and many others of a similar character might be added:

"In the earlier part of my ministry I was frequently thrown with Mr. P. and we conversed freely on many topics about which we differed. He had spoken very plainly to me but I had not thought of taking offence. One night we were guests of the same family, while attending the session of an Association; and as we were walking out together after supper, he turned suddenly to me and said: 'I have been thinking of what has passed between us, and I have feared that at some time I may have wounded your feelings by my plainness of speech. If so I did not intend it and I wish to ask your pardon.'"

"This to a mere youth, from one so far above me in every respect, both surprised and humbled me, while it raised still higher my already exalted estimate of the man."

His whole life demonstrates his strength of will and firmness of purpose. An undertaking once entered upon, he prosecuted it with unfaltering energy. Failure did not discourage him. Again and again he returned to the work, his courage and his resources rising with the emergency, till at last opposition gave way and victory crowned his efforts.

Of poetic imagination he had but little; of poetic feeling a great deal. The grand and the beautiful in nature, and the nobler qualities of the heart, manifested in the scenes of real life, affected him deeply. In his friendships, in his ministerial labors and within the sacred precincts of home, he evinced much of the tenderness, patience, constancy and firmness with which writers of fiction delight to invest their heroes.

His heart was keenly alive to all the claims of humanity. Whether he sat by the bedside of the sick and dying and pointed them to the Saviour of sinners, or visited the sorrowing and the bereaved, or entered the abodes of the poor and wretched, or mingled in the brighter scenes of social enjoyment, his warm heart and active sympathies prepared him for the task and rendered him ever a welcome guest.

To his natural endowments of head and heart Grace had imparted its ennobling and beautifying influence. His religious experience was clearly marked, and his piety intelligent, earnest, active and consistent. He had, on the one hand, a lively sense of his need of the Saviour, and, on the other, an unwavering confidence in the all-sufficiency of Christ. Hence, while he was always humble he was always cheerful.

He was a consecrated man. Himself and all that he possessed, he had given to the Lord. When a friend advised him to read a popular novel he replied, "I have never read a novel. I can not spend my time in reading such things when there is so much to do for God." His time, he felt, was not his own. So with his children. When they were sick his prayer was: "O God, spare them, for *thyself first;* then for *usefulness in the world;* then for us."

He recognized fully the doctrine of a special Providence—saw in everything a Father's hand, directing, restraining, controlling—and as a consequence he was a man of prayer. Said one who knew him well: "I do not remember a single instance of Mr. P's. retiring at night without first returning thanks for mercies received and invoking a continuance of the same. After traveling all day, or mingling with his brethren in the deliberations of religious bodies, no matter how much exhausted he was at night, he would say to his room mates: 'Let us ask God's blessing before we retire.' And kneeling at his bedside he would lead us in prayer or request one of the company to do it."

His views in reference to benevolent enterprises were enlightened and liberal. He could not be localized and he had no hobbies. He was the ardent friend and promoter of Home Missions but equally zealous as an advocate of Foreign Missions and Education. Whatever had for its object to build up the Redeemer's kingdom found in him a cordial friend. As a preacher he stood high. His sermons were carefully and prayerfully prepared. His favorite themes were the great truths of the Gospel, such as Justification by Faith, the Imputation of Christ's Righteousness, Election, &c., &c. His style was plain and his manner simple but earnest. He was careful to fortify every position which he took, with testimony from the Scriptures. He gathered illustrations from a great variety of sources and used them freely and often with great effect. In the ordinary acceptation of the term he was not an eloquent preacher, and yet at times, as he discussed some of the grand truths of the New Testament and warmed with his subject, there was about him a sort of eloquence that made him almost irresistible.

It is needless to speak of him as a pastor. The living fruits of his labors tell, better than we can, his capacity and faithfulness in this important sphere of usefulness. In the domestic circle, he ever aimed to promote the happiness of each individual. By constant acts of attention, trivial in themselves, he sought to add to the comfort of his household—to lessen the cares of the elder members and increase the pleasures of the younger. Many tender allusions to the "dear children," in his diary, as he planned various amusements for the little ones, or furnished some interesting book or magazine to the older children, show what a devoted father he was. Whatever strictness appeared in his discipline, was only caused by his earnest desire to have his children examples of goodness. While he commanded their respect and implicit obedience, their affection for him was not the less. "Papa's study" was always a favorite resort for the little ones, to enjoy a quiet play, or look at the pictures in his books, which he always permitted them to use, saying: "They would be less apt to *abuse* books, if accustomed to the *use* of them." "My children, never disturb me," he would say, "when goodnaturedly playing;" and he loved to have them with him, even when writing and studying. Indeed, they early learned to restrain the exuberance of playful feeling, while "Papa was studying his sermon."

Said one of his little sons, while speaking of the pleasant hours he had spent here with his father: "Papa always used to pray before he commenced studying his sermon and we used to kneel down with him." Feeling, as he did, the want of early educational advantages, he afforded his children every opportunity for mental culture. By sending them to the best schools, and supplying them with useful and entertaining reading, he encouraged the love of books which they early manifested. "What would I not have given when I was your age," he would tell them, "for the books and periodicals you have access to?" That his children might, "if possible, receive a good education," was the only special request he left in reference to their future management. But above every thing else, as has been said, he desired that they might become holy men and women, and from their earliest infancy they were specially dedicated to God in prayer. The regular observance of family worship was deemed by him an important measure for promoting piety; and this service, instead of being a cold, unmeaning formality, was rendered interesting to every member of the family by requiring each to share in its exercises. His children will never forget the "first verse" they learned to repeat at morning prayers. After a passage of Scripture was repeated by each member of the family, all joined in reading a chapter and singing a hymn. Then followed a prayer suited to the peculiar condition of the family. This was the order of exercises for the morning. At night they were somewhat shorter in order that the younger children might retire early. In these family devotions the New Testament was read many times through, and the whole Bible once or twice.

When Mr. P. was at home nothing was ever allowed to prevent family worship. On several occasions, when confined to his bed by sickness, the family assembled in his chamber, at the appointed hour, and after the chapter for the day had been read, he led the devotions while all bowed around him.

One incident may be related in this connection. On the morning of the 3rd of August, 1856, all had assembled for prayers. Little Jemmie, after a night of great suffering, lay quiet in his cradle. When the others had repeated their verses of Scripture, Mr. P. turned to little J. and said: "My son, can you say your verse for papa?" Some who were present seemed surprised at the question, supposing the child unconscious of what was passing. But without the slightest hesitation he distinctly repeated one of the last verses he had learned: "As the mountains are round about Jerusalem, so the Lord is round about his people from henceforth, even forever."

How touching and appropriate was this precious promise to these parents as repeated by their dying child. In after years, as memory recalled that passage, so impressively uttered, it seemed to them like a message of comfort from heaven.

Mr. Prichard's influence could not but be widely felt. The preceding pages show, to some extent, what it was. One phase of it, which has not been referred to, demands a passing notice. The story of his early struggles was extensively known in his native State and in other States; and it has awakened in more than one heart aspirations for the advantages which education gives, and a stern resolve to obtain them. Some of those who, toiling on in poverty and ignorance, caught their first gleam of hope from his example, and afterwards rose to honor and usefulness, are known to the writer. The full influence of that example will be known only in eternity.

This survey will be closed by a reference to Mr. Prichard's character and influence by one of his Virginia brethren, who knew him intimately:

"Though I am conscious of inability to speak of him as I feel, I shall aim to give my impression as to the more salient points of his character. He was by nature, a noble spirit, generous, affectionate and courageous. His will was strong, his feelings intense, and his moral tone pure and lofty. When he gave himself to Christ, the consecration was entire; and love to an unseen Saviour was thenceforth the motive power, the guiding and controlling principle of his life.

"His disposition was eminently social, and he seemed never happier than when surrounded by congenial brethren in his own hospitable home. Were these brethren less cultivated or experienced than himself, he would, when the occasion demanded, kindly and unassumingly extend to them the benefits of his superior attainments. If, on the other hand, his companions were men more able than himself, he regarded them with an admiration unmixed with envy, and would gladly sit as a learner at their feet. But these sentiments never degenerated into a cringing deference to their opinions, when those opinions did not commend themselves to his own judgment; and whenever he differed with others, no mock modesty prevented him from frankly expressing his dissent. Still less was he ever restrained by fear, an emotion of which, I believe, he was experimentally ignorant. If, as sometimes happened, he encountered an opponent as fearless and as decided as himself, long and sharp word battles might ensue; but, on his part certainly, they were never accompanied or followed by a trace of wounded feeling; while he never intentionally gave occasion for such feeling to the other party.

"While he would not have been deemed an imprudent man, he was, less than most men, restrained and influenced by motives of expediency. If honor or justice seemed to indicate a certain course, he never stopped to consider whether it was popular or likely to succeed; but promptly entered upon it, and unhesitatingly pursued it to the bitter end.

He thus, at times, doubtless incurred the disapprobation and the dislike of some persons; but if they knew him at all, and were possessed of ordinary candor, they could not fail to admire his noble independence—his almost sublime abandonment to what he thought.

"I will cite an instance in illustration of this point. It has long been the rule of the Virginia Baptist Education Board, to require of each beneficiary a bond for the amount furnished him, payable, however, only when he should feel himself able to pay it. Mr. Prichard was opposed to this plan. He had lively recollections of his own experience in securing an education, and his sympathy for the student for the ministry had almost a motherly tenderness. Hence, while no man on earth would have been prompter or more certain to pay such a claim, he yet thought that it ought not, even in the mildest form, to be held over the young minister; but that the churches should send him forth to his work, debt-free.

"Well do I remember the earnestness with which, at a meeting of the Society held at the 2nd Baptist Church, Richmond, nearly twenty years ago, he attacked the rule which has been mentioned. Several noble young men, beneficiaries, were sitting near me in the gallery, and manifested deep emotion at his warm championship in their behalf. He was unsuccessful, and some annoyance may have been felt at his persistence, by those whose policy he opposed; but in after years, again and again, when the subject came up, he would urge his protest.

"His mind was not what would be called of the logical order, and he had not enjoyed the advantage of an early and the most thorough training. His conclusions seemed to be often rather the result of intuition than of reasoning; but if this was so, his intuitions were certainly remarkable for their acuteness, and his conclusions for their accuracy. His thoughts were the effect rather than the cause of his emotions; and when some strong feeling stirred his heart, his mind often flashed with the corruscations of genius.

"On this account, as might have been anticipated, his pulpit efforts were peculiarly unequal. Though he was a hard student, and specially in his later years was generally instructive, yet as he was not a Biblical critic, nor a great reasoner, his sermons, when he lacked the inspiration of deep feeling, may not have been powerful; but when his heart was glowing, when his sensibilities were aroused and the surroundings were favorable to the play of his emotional nature;—then, he was truly eloquent, carrying his audience away by his appeals or melting them by his pathos. Hence, he probably never did himself justice in his efforts in "strange cities," or on occasions when he conceived himself surrounded by the unappreciative or the critical. The presence of such a congregation, while it inspired no fear, chilled him, and rendered impossible that mysterious sympathy so essential to effective speaking. But with his own people, of whose appreciation he felt sure, or at some Association, where he was perfectly at home, he often felt the divine afflatus, and his discourses were characterized by that highest of all qualities in the pulpit—that blended fervor and tenderness which constitute what we call *unction*.

"I shall never forget a familiar sermon which I heard him preach in his Lecture-room in Lynchburg, in '52 or '53, from Phil. IV: 6, 7. Perhaps no new truth was brought to light; but, as with a deep and quiet tone, he unfolded the precious contents of the text, an almost painful stillness prevailed, and many eyes were swimming in tears. Specially do I remember how he dwelt on the fact that it was through Christ that the believer enjoys the promised peace. "Jesus, that name—that golden key which unlocks to us the store house of gospel blessings:" these words, and the amplification of the idea, were presented within describable pathos, and produced an effect that was thrilling.

"The secret of his preaching was also the secret of the influence which he exerted. This influence was strictly personal, and was due to the sympathetic power of his genial yet decided and positive character. More than by his arguments, he was by his pure life, and his pious spirit, a motor for good, a leader of his fellow men into the paths of truth and righteousness.

"Among his minor yet distinctive traits of character, was the intense love that he felt for his mother state—his strong State pride. He loved the very dust of North Carolina, and would have resented any imputation upon her honor more warmly than a personal affront. This trait, however, co-existed with as enlarged a catholicity as I ever saw in any man. His heart was too big, both by nature and by grace, not to love ardently every good object, every lovable person, whenever found. I am reminded that the last time I saw him was in the Summer of 1862, when he came to Richmond to visit the sick and wounded North Carolina soldiers who were in the hospitals in that city. It was to him, in a three fold sense, a labor of love; and day after day, despite the enervating sun, and his own feebleness, he ministered to their temporal and eternal wants.

"Indulge me in a word as to the circumstances of his death. He died nobly. Unstimulated by the excitements of the battle field, he stood firmly at his post, amid the raging epidemic, earnestly working, patiently waiting, and calmly looking death in the face. All have applauded the heroism of his course and the purity of his motives; but some may have regarded his remaining in Wilmington as a needless and a wrong exposure. I cannot so regard it. I do not blame any man who, in similar circumstances, feels called upon to leave his post. It is a matter which every one must decide for himself; but he who elects to 'stand and wait,' though 'plagues and deaths around him fly,' seems to me to have 'chosen the better part.'

"In the prevalence of a fatal epidemic, it would indeed be well, if the entire population could be removed from the infected regions, that the fuel being removed the fire might die. But it is seldom that this is possible. Various causes may render it necessary for many to remain. Generally speaking, the bulk of a church—mainly poor people—do not and cannot get away. The pastor, who voluntarily forbears to avail himself of his opportunity to go, and of his own accord remains with the many who cannot leave, sharing the perils and troubles which he might avoid, seems to me eminently acting in the spirit of Him, who, possessed of infinite power, forebore to use it for his own good, but shared the lot of the lowly and the poor whom he came to save. And if such a pastor falls under such circumstances, verily, he 'falls, a blessed martyr.' His last labors may be, in every sense, his best, and from his fall more good may follow than a prolonged life could have secured. I rejoice that Pastors, as well as Priests, are ready to minister in the infected hospital and on the bloody battle field, though the former do not lay the stress, that the latter do, upon ministrations performed for the dying and for the dead."

First Baptist Church, the construc-
tion which Rev. Prichard oversaw,
as it appeared in the early 1900's.

Photo courtesy New Hanover County Public Library.

If you enjoyed this book,
check out more great
Cape Fear and North Carolina
history titles at

www.dramtreebooks.com.

We tell the stories that tell the
North Carolina story!

Printed in the United States
76822LV00002B/1-48

9 780978 624880

ML 4/08